AF251003

ART AND THE RIVER

Views and Visions of the Housatonic

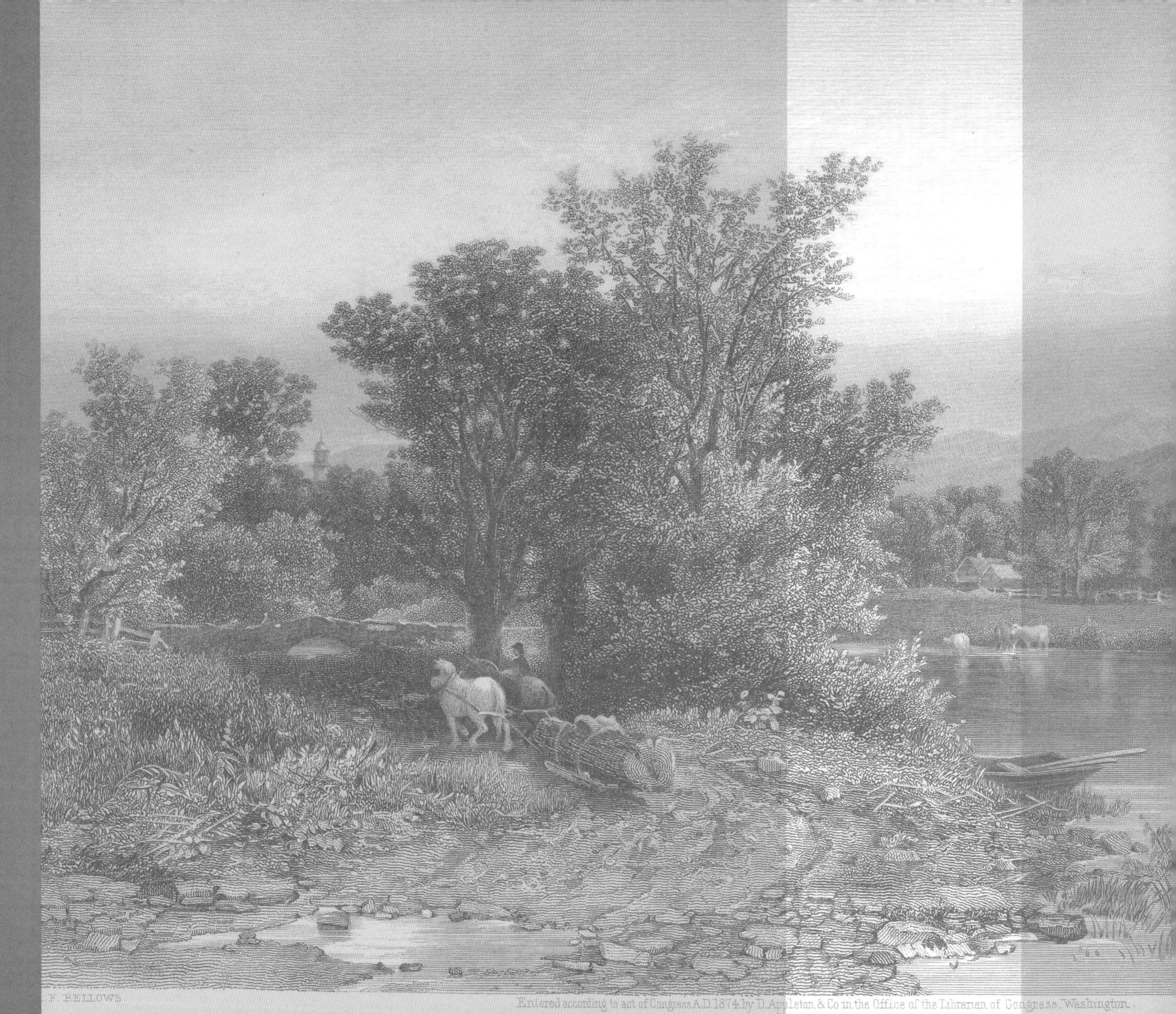
F. BELLOWS
Entered according to act of Congress A.D. 1874 by D.Appleton & Co in the Office of the Librarian of Congress Washington.

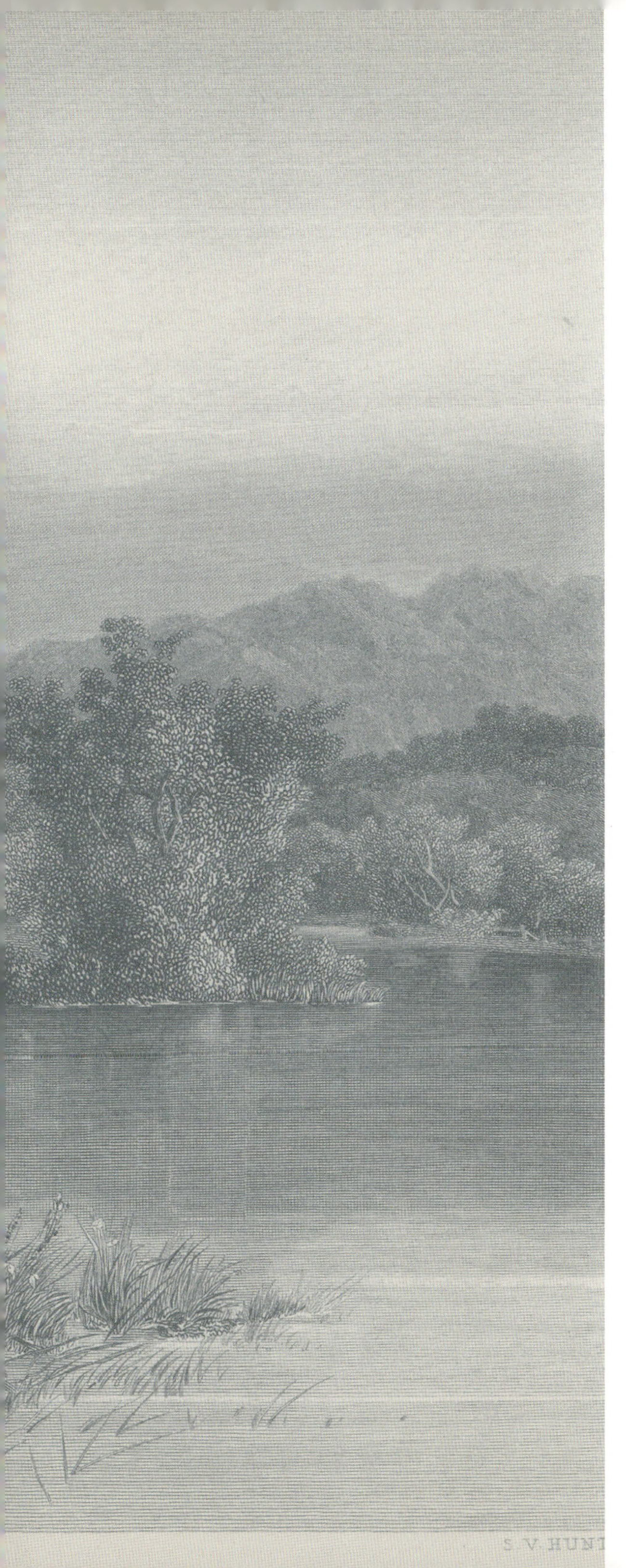

ART AND THE RIVER

Views and Visions of the Housatonic

Nancy Goldberger
& Andrea Scott, editors

Sheffield Art League Great Barrington, Massachusetts

Editors   Nancy Goldberger and Andrea Scott

Designer   Jennifer Clark

Scans and maps   Barbara Winters

Published by the Sheffield Art League
Box 296
Great Barrington, Massachusetts 01230
www.SheffieldArtLeague.org

Printing: Excelsior Printing Co., North Adams, Massachusetts

This book was published as part of the Sheffield Art League's Housatonic River
Summer 2004, a community celebration of the Housatonic River in
Massachusetts and northwest Connecticut. More than 30 art, conservancy,
cultural, and educational organizations were co-sponsors of this celebration.
www.HousatonicRiverSummer.org

Map on pages 10 and 11: Original cartography from Massachusetts Atlas and
Gazetteer and Connecticut/Rhode Island Atlas and Gazetteer. Used with
permission of the publisher. © Copyright DeLorme, Yarmouth, ME 04096

© Arshile Gorky *Golden Brown*, 2004 Artists Rights Society (ARS), New York

Printed in the U.S.A.

ISBN 0-9749919-0-2 (Cloth)
ISBN 0-9749919-1-0 (Paper)

Cover: **Housatonic Falls, Falls Village** by J.D. Woodward from "Picturesque
America," Volume 2 (1874), William Cullen Bryant, editor. **Scene on the
Housatonic River** (c. 1885) by Arthur Parton.

CONTENTS

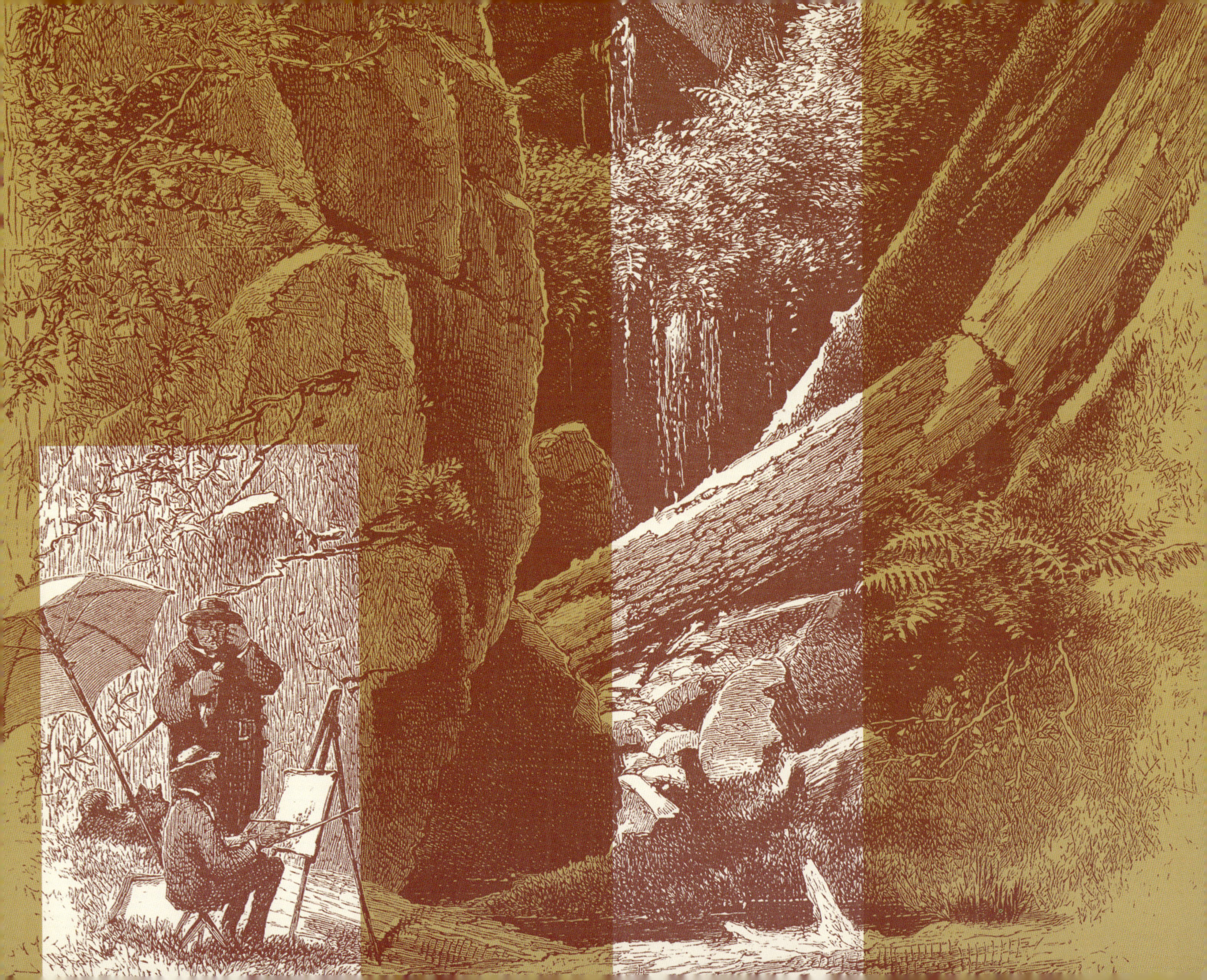

FOREWORD

I love the river. A tiny tributary that ultimately feeds into the Housatonic runs down the mountain behind my house. I have driven along the river many times on my way here and there and often stopped to watch the rush of the water and the light play around the foliage along its banks. With luck, I spot blue herons and kingfishers. I have canoed the river and taken walks at Bartholomew's Cobble. Hidden pools in some of the Housatonic's tributaries—clear and safe from pollution—have beckoned me on hot summer days. Driving down Route 7 in Connecticut, I always catch my breath when I see the river widen and open up to distant vistas. As an artist, I have painted images of the river—the invasive but gorgeous purple loosestrife that appears in late summer, the smokestacks of the Rising Paper Company that dominate a particular view of the river as it moves through my town of Housatonic, the seasonal, changing colors of the river from a bridge in Sheffield.

Ever since the Berkshires and the Litchfield Hills were first settled, the upper Housatonic River from the headwaters near Pittsfield, Massachusetts, to Kent, Connecticut, has been an attraction for artists as well as a waterway that linked the river communities. Nineteenth-century painters beautifully recorded the river's bucolic surroundings; today, remnants of dams, mills, iron furnaces, and other signs of industry along its banks remind us of the river as a source of energy—and of the destructiveness of human intrusion during most of the twentieth century.

Contemporary artists of the Housatonic River respond to the same impulse that motivated their nineteeth-century predecessors. Artists' sense of nature and sense of place bring them to the riverbank with easels and cameras. What they create transforms the way we see the landscape around us, which takes hold in the imagination. Artists thus can help communities create a collective vision that prizes the landscape, a vision that can turn into a powerful force for protecting natural resources, especially when combined with the work of conservationists.

In the spring of 2003, when my Sheffield Art League colleague Bill Connell first suggested that we plan a celebration of the river's future by bringing together artists and river conservationists, I enthusiastically agreed. Thanks to river cleanups over the past few decades and some individuals devoted to its rescue, the Housatonic River is moving from a spoiled past into a new future as a source of inspiration. The idea of community organizations coming together to sponsor a series of art and river events began to take shape. With the Sheffield Art League taking the lead, more than 30 non-profit art, educational, cultural, and conservancy organizations from Berkshire and Litchfield counties joined to create Housatonic River Summer 2004.

As part of the summer's program, the Sheffield Art League, together with the Norman Rockwell Museum, Chesterwood

Museum, Simon's Rock College, and Sculpture Now, sponsored five juried shows covering framed art, photography, and sculpture. We put out a call to artists in the Berkshires and beyond to submit work inspired by the Housatonic River, its tributaries, and its flora and fauna. These art shows, along with a host of river events, festival days, lectures on the river's past and present, concerts of river music, performances, river flotilla, and other forms of celebration, brought the community's attention to both the past and future of the river.

To commemorate that celebration and spirit, the Sheffield Art League is publishing this book. It includes images of the river by historic and well-known contemporary artists, with commentary by an art historian and a contemporary art specialist. It includes historians and conservationists speaking about the river's long history and ongoing rescue. We hope that *Art and the River: Views and Visions of the Housatonic* will serve as a souvenir of the summer's events and of our community's celebration of a treasured natural resource, the Housatonic River.

NANCY GOLDBERGER
President, Sheffield Art League
Co-Director, Housatonic River Summer 2004

ACKNOWLEDGMENTS

To all the many people and organizations who have worked to make Housatonic River Summer 2004 a success, may this book be a reminder of the power of collaboration in reaching common goals. From the first days of brainstorming and setting the objectives for the project to the hard work of committees and event planning, the spirit of the volunteers has been extraordinary. Blessings upon you all.

The people behind this book deserve attention at this point. The Sheffield Art League Board of Directors and members are to be applauded for sponsoring HRS2004 and for overseeing the production and distribution of *Art and the River: Views and Visions of the Housatonic*. Special thanks to Jane and Jack Fitzpatrick and the High Meadow Foundation, Frelinghuysen Morris House and Studio, Emily and John Alexander, Lila Berle, the Hickey Family Foundation, and the Board of the proposed Upper Housatonic National Heritage Area for making this book possible. Without their generous support, we could not have begun to put such a book together.

Lila Berle, Maureen Hickey, and I were the instrumental dreamers whose visions launched this project. Robert Austin pointed us to the rich history of artists in the Litchfield Hills. The images of the artists and the words of the essayists in this book indelibly portray the heart and soul of the river. The enthusiasm and creative energy of the production team brought the book to life: Andrea Scott, my co-editor; Jennifer Clark, book designer; Barbara Winters, map and art reproduction; Maia Falconi-Sachs, our design intern. Geoffrey Young, Mike Levitas, and Leo Goldberger provided wise advice on both visual and editorial matters. Cia Elkin and Jill Jakes gave later drafts a close reading. Finally, thanks to Gerry Harding/Excelsior Printing, whose guidance turned this book into a beauty.

NANCY GOLDBERGER

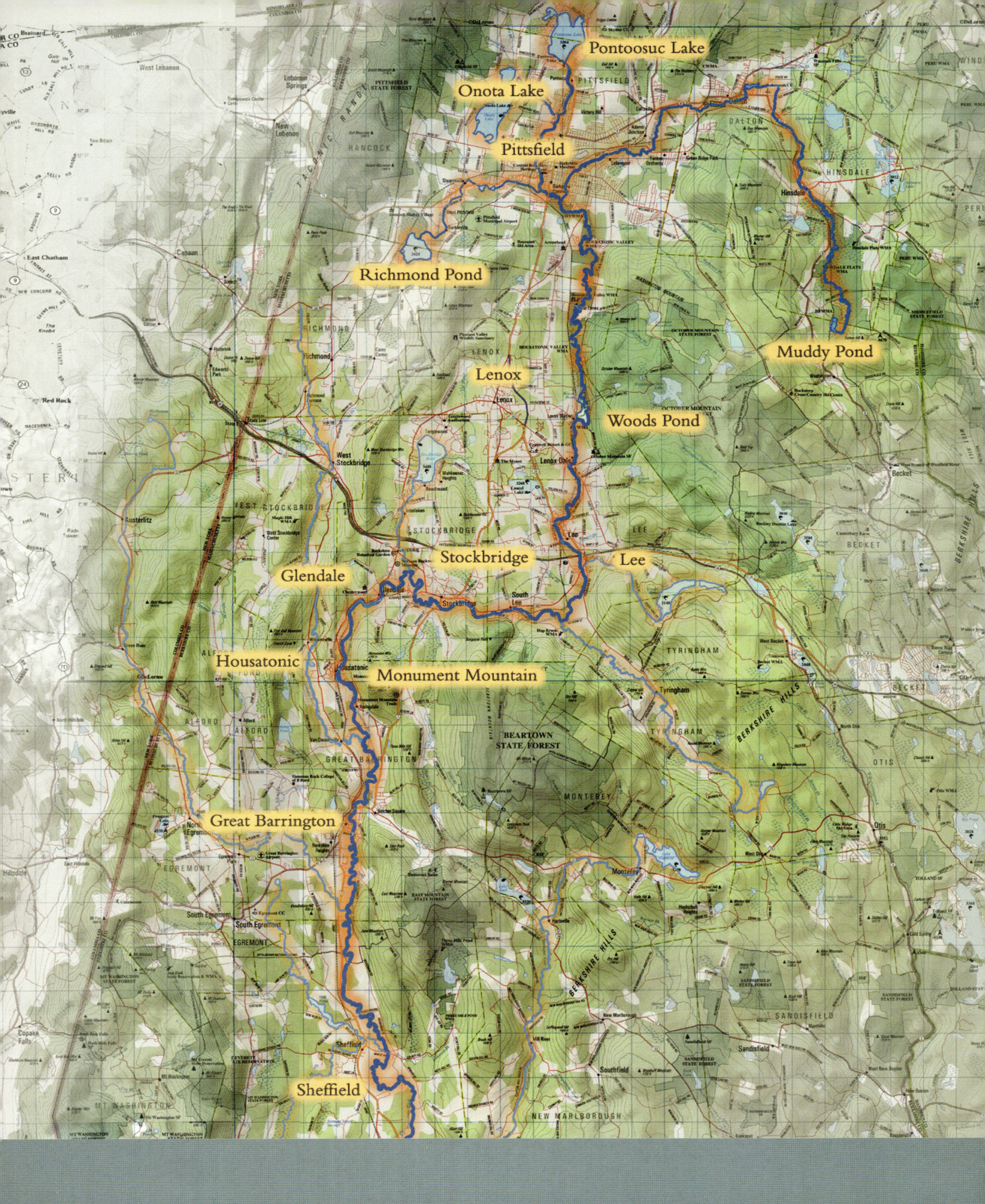

Pontoosuc Lake
Onota Lake
Pittsfield
Richmond Pond
Muddy Pond
Lenox
Woods Pond
Stockbridge
Lee
Glendale
Housatonic
Monument Mountain
Great Barrington
Sheffield

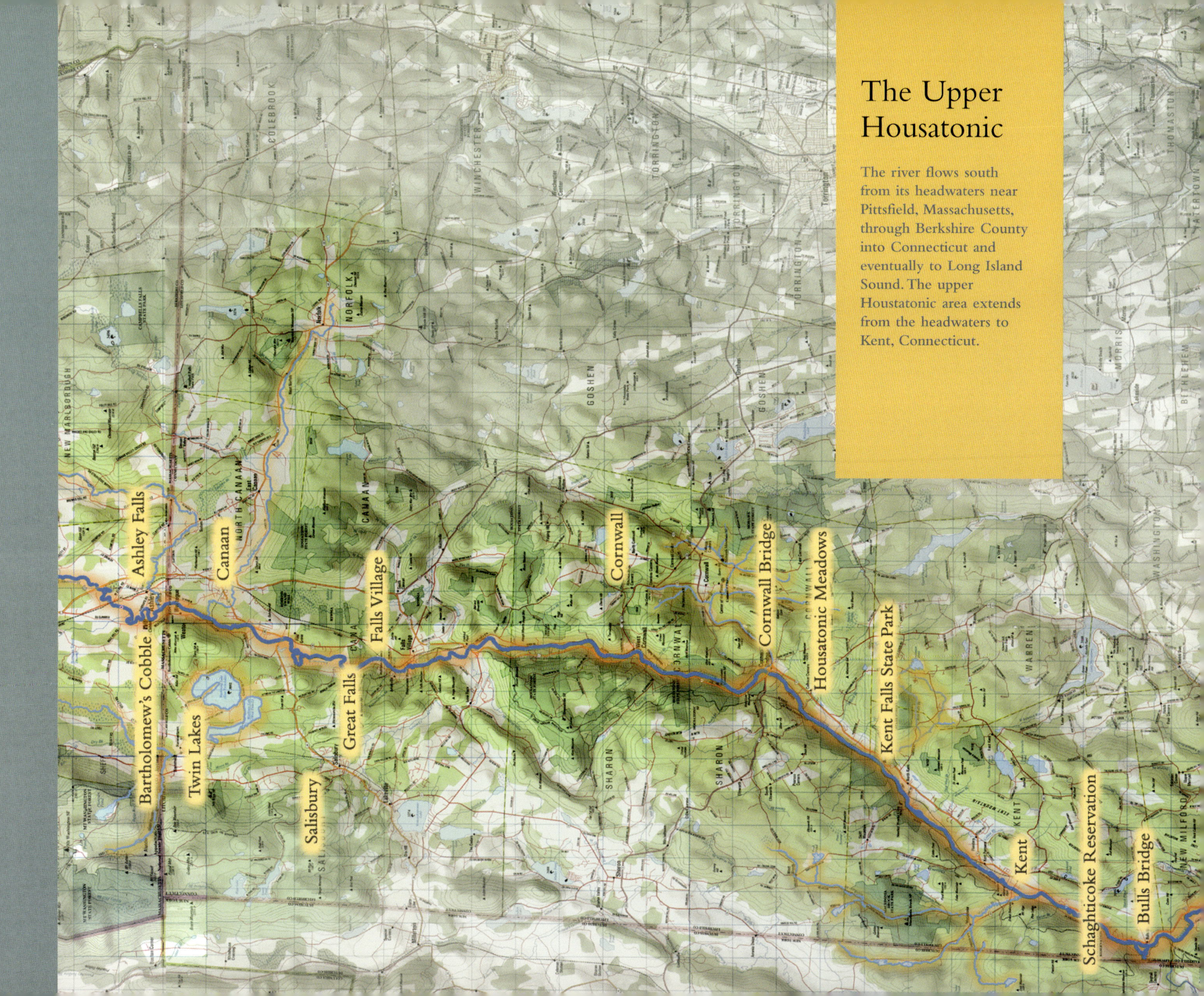

The Upper Housatonic

The river flows south from its headwaters near Pittsfield, Massachusetts, through Berkshire County into Connecticut and eventually to Long Island Sound. The upper Houstatonic area extends from the headwaters to Kent, Connecticut.

Ashley Falls
Canaan
Bartholomew's Cobble
Twin Lakes
Salisbury
Great Falls
Falls Village
Cornwall
Cornwall Bridge
Housatonic Meadows
Kent Falls State Park
Kent
Schaghticoke Reservation
Bulls Bridge

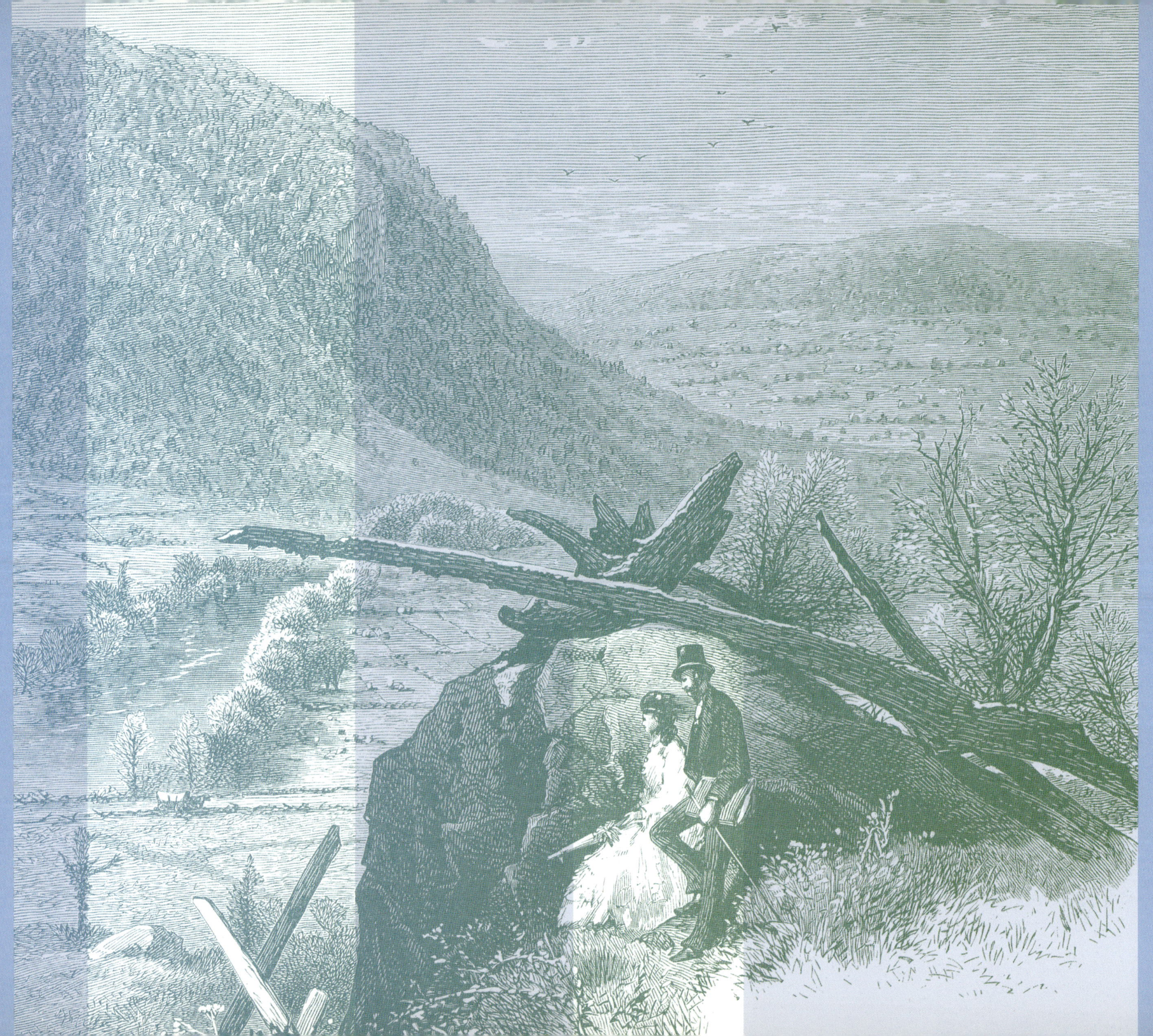

THE COURSE OF THE HOUSATONIC

Richard Nunley

Richard Nunley wrote a weekly column in The Berkshire Eagle for more than 20 years. He edited "The Berkshire Reader" and wrote accompanying text for "Spirit of Nature," a book of Jim Schantz's paintings, from which this essay is adapted.

The name Housatonic derives from the Mahican Wussi-adene-uk—beyond-the-mountain-place or Place Beyond the Mountain. Wussi-adene-uk through usage eroded into Wusatenuk, which whites had spelled variously—Westenhook, Hooestennuc, Ousetomunkc, Housatunack, Housatonic. Originally the name of the region as a whole, over time Housatonic became the name of the river itself.

The Housatonic is the principal river between the Connecticut and the Hudson, although it is a much shorter and smaller, and hence more intimately scaled, stream than either of those two grander waterways.

This rural river begins within the city of Pittsfield, Massachusetts, where its three main tributary branches come together. The Middle Branch, which once powered a series of textile mills, flows out of Pontoosuc Lake, which collects the drainage from the southwest slopes of Mount Greylock, the highest point in Massachusetts.

The East Branch rises in Muddy Pond in the town of Washington, high on the forested spine of the Berkshire Hills; and on its winding way northward to Pittsfield passes the paper mills of Crane and Co., in Dalton, where, along with a variety of other fine paper products, the paper for U.S. currency is manufactured.

The Southwest Branch flows out of Richmond Pond and is augmented by Shaker Brook, a brawling mountain stream that comes down from Lebanon Mountain and passes through the ordered neatness of Hancock Shaker Village and its pleasant agricultural levels.

From the time of the area's earliest settlement in the later decades of the eighteenth century, the Housatonic and its tributaries have been harnessed for power—small grist mills and sawmills at first, and then, as industrialism accelerated, paper mills, wool and cotton mills, shoe and machine tool factories, blast furnaces and iron foundries, quarries and glass works, each generation's successively larger than the last. Then water power waned as preferable energy sources became available, though the river still is used to generate electrical power in Connecticut.

As a result of the evolving periods of industrial activity, today's Housatonic flows through identifiable phases of the built past—sleepy quaint hamlets, settled picturesque towns, small brick cities that are being rediscovered by tourists and weekenders from New York and Boston because of the attractive small-town authenticity.

Thanks to its past as a working river, the Housatonic on its rambling course passes innumerable foundations of vanished mills overgrown with brambles, bushes, and trees. It flows past the stone blocks of bridge piers or breached dams, and in places is paralleled by dry millraces where leaves and rubbish collect. Now and then it comes upon still-standing clock-towered factories, some of astonishing size.

These evidences of industry notwithstanding, the Housatonic is essentially a rural stream. Even where it flows through built-up areas, it is usually behind or under things, unnoticed and undisturbed. Its banks are often bordered by thickets or woods of maple and cherry strung with grapevines or bittersweet, the haunt of skunks and raccoons, ducks and deer. In Berkshire County, even when it becomes urban, it is soon out in the country again, meandering as if preoccupied through its flood plain of wide meadows, cornfields, woods, and pastures, a mostly sluggish river now widening into a rush-fringed pond, now hastening a little where hills crowd in and narrow it, now changing its mind where a mountain in the way deflects it from its generally southerly course to do a leisurely loop around three quarters of the compass—a complaisant river serenely confident of arriving somewhere, sometime. In Litchfield County, the Housatonic grows more urgent, flowing more steeply through a valley it cut out of marble, the tributary streams tumbling down and the river itself (when not harnessed by the power company) crashing over water-smoothed rock at the Great Falls in Falls Village. By the time it reaches Kent, the river has gone back to its meandering ways, then plummets through Bulls Bridge Gorge and heads to Long Island Sound.

It is the jumbled terrain the Housatonic works its way through—the flanking ranges of the Berkshires to the east and the Taconics to the west, the lumps of Litchfield Hills, the masses of steeps like Monument Mountain and the lesser hills and ridges that intrude into valley—that creates the continually changing vistas of the lovely and the wild that have charmed artists (and their patrons) no less than writers and tourists. From the summit of Mount Greylock, the summer view south over Berkshire County looks like a green carpet spread over a very lumpy floor, with puddles of blue lakes here and there in its folds.

Through this terrain the river maintains a space open to the ever-changing sky and directs the vision into a view of cows and a village where the river bends, or of trees framing lordly mountain profiles in the distance—images of the nostalgic or the sublime.

Thomas Cole, Asher Durand, Alfred Fitch Bellows, George Inness, Frederick Church, John Kensett, William S. Haseltine, Aaron Shattuck, Samuel Colman, Christopher P. Cranch, Arthur Parton, John Bristol, Abbott Thayer, Hugh Bolton Jones, Rockwell Kent, John Marin, Fairfield Porter—all these and more came to paint the Housatonic landscape, finding in its natural beauty images of an elevating serenity that grips the spirit.

FISHING THE KONKAPOT

John Manikowski

John Manikowski, outdoorsman, cook, wildlife and landscape artist, came to the Berkshires in 1972. He often writes and illustrates for Field and Stream. The Konkapot is a tributary of the Housatonic that flows near his home in Mill River, Massachusetts.

I stand equidistant between the wild roar of a waterfall and—behind and below me, in harmonious contrast—the refreshing din of a gurgling stream. A fringed blue sky slips behind an orange scrim, creating a pleasantly diffused hue suitable for evening trout fishing. Here, the water pursues its lowest point, listlessly wandering. The dither of chickadees diminishes beneath the tympanic rasping of crusty bullfrogs. Broadleaf skunk cabbage carpets the riverbank shielded by spindly horsetail shoots, wild grape and bittersweet vines, young beech and red oak saplings. A short cast away, moss-gloved rocks quiver on the shoreline.

I maneuver around slate bedrock, bulldozed into place some 15,000 years ago under glacial movement. In diligent pursuit, I head upstream as I have heard rumors concerning the appetite of a notable brown trout that may

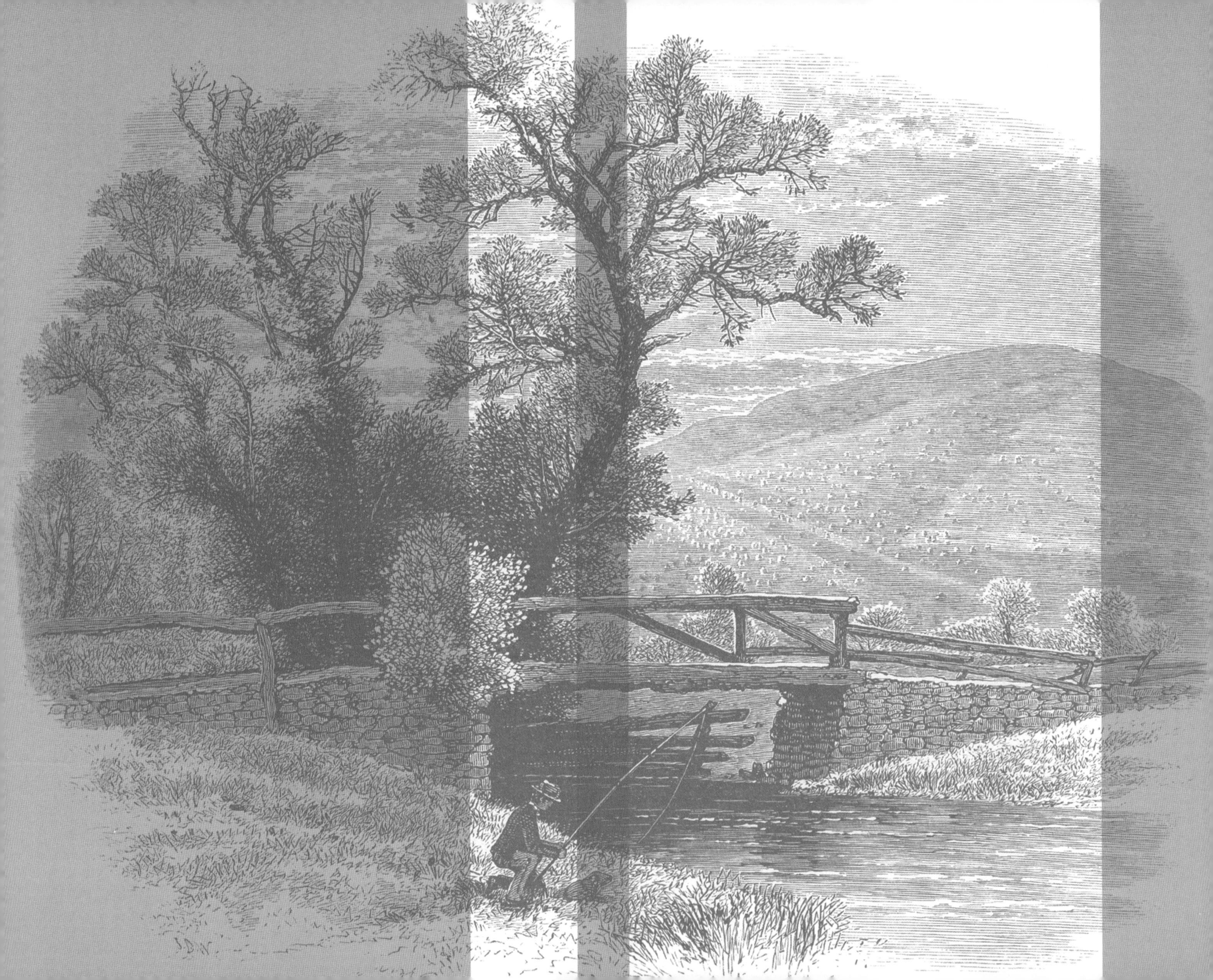

be lurking under cover of a more recently submerged stone, a millstone. Quietly, I wade over to a favorite pool on the Konkapot River, the cooling waters flowing through man-made, sculpted stone monoliths of what was once the Crosby & Robbins paper mill, just up from the Hayes Hill bridge.

Nearly two and a half centuries ago, this meandering stretch of water spawned more than one dozen mills that lined a mere 1.3 miles of the river! Here, energy was unleashed in waterpower that still courses this limestone-rich corridor. With the help of grist wheels that ground wheat into flour, cut trees into lumber, and turned pulp into paper, the village of Mill River hummed. But now, the chiseled viaducts and foundations stand camouflaged under shrubby brush and bush, idle, stone footprints—reminders of a river-life long ago. The sun dips without fanfare behind the lee side of Brush Hill, casting no shadow on the water; ideal fishing terms.

Downstream, I watch the current rip my fly through riffle and eddy over bricks worn smooth from centuries of immersion, the dimly visible red clay hinting at sumac's premature changeover to fall.

I am silenced by the beauty of a river still richly textured, bisecting a mill town alive with working memories. I am in awe of the river power that once turned massive stone cogwheels, methodically, patiently, sculpting its own sluiceways through bedrock, thrashing against quartzite oxbows.

A few moments later, a wary trout dashes up to a protective niche beneath an ancient millstone; seeking shelter, home. I am home, too, in the belly of the Konkapot. In the belly of history.

A dozen of the brooks, streams, rivulets, and rivers that feed the Housatonic in western Massachusetts and northwestern Connecticut

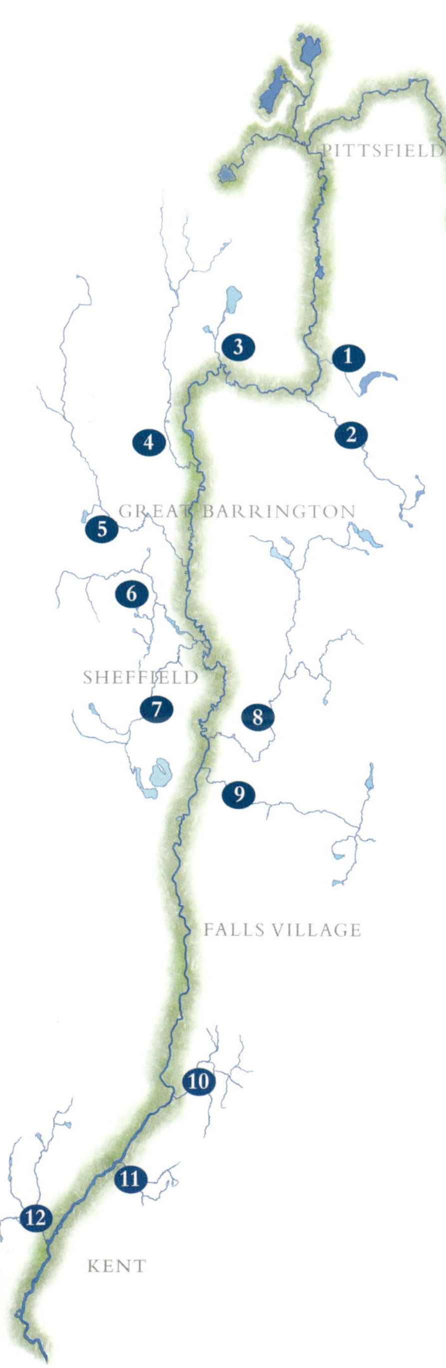

Tributaries of the Housatonic

1 Goose Pond Brook
2 Hop Brook
3 Larrywaug Brook
4 Williams River
5 Green River
6 Hubbard Brook
7 Schenob Brook
8 Konkapot River
9 Blackberry River
10 Furnace Brook
11 Kent Falls Brook
12 Macedonia Brook

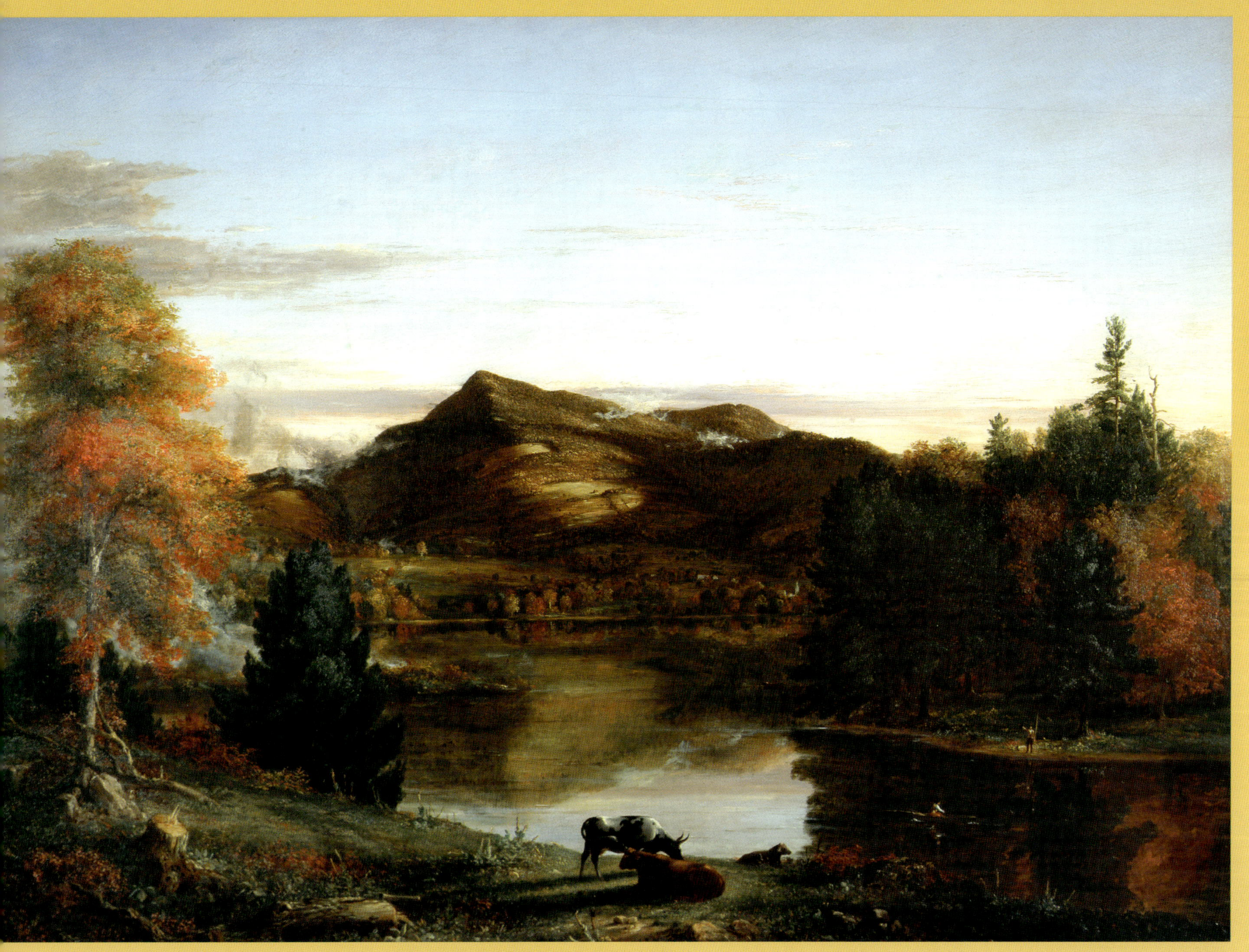

A PARADISE OF PAINTERS

Maureen Hickey

Maureen Hickey holds a doctorate in museum education and American art history. She has curated several exhibits focused on Berkshire-inspired art and is currently working on a show for the Clark Art Institute about George Inness and his Berkshire patrons.

Thomas Cole
View of Hoosac Mountain and Pontoosuc Lake Near Pittsfield, Massachusetts

Nearly every eminent American landscape painter of the nineteenth and early twentieth centuries, and many others who enjoyed lesser acclaim, painted in the Berkshires or the Litchfield Hills. The distinctive geography, with its tracts of wilderness, fields, and pastures set off by rolling hills and small mountains and watered by the Housatonic River and its streams, made it an inspiring place to work, "a place by itself," as a travel writer put it in 1885.

Herman Melville described the midsummer activity near his Pittsfield farmhouse in 1856: "The country…was such a picture, that in berry time no boy climbs hills or crosses vales without coming upon easels planted in every nook, and sunburnt painters there. A very paradise of painters."

In addition to a landscape where the lovely and the wild

mingled in harmony, as William Cullen Bryant put it, the region was rich in potential patrons. From the 1830s on, the upper Housatonic region attracted artists, writers, intellectuals, moralists, tourists, and some of the nation's wealthiest entrepreneurs. Most were seasonal refugees from the city who sought in the region's picturesque scenery and refined society a return to Arcadia, the place that provided safe haven from the disorders of civilization.

Soon after America gained its independence, writers such as Alexis de Tocqueville, Henry David Thoreau, and Ralph Waldo Emerson had started to write about those disorders and the destruction of the American land. Other writers, such as Henry Wadsworth Longfellow, Henry Ward Beecher, and especially William Cullen Bryant, found the scenic Arcadian beauty of the Housatonic valley the perfect retreat. They praised its mountains, streams, fields, and the winding river as an idyllic region where one could live in balance with nature.

Bryant, one of the most powerful literary figures in the nineteenth century, had settled in Great Barrington in 1816. He became an ardent promoter of the Berkshires and the Litchfield Hills. In his book "Picturesque America" (1874), he described the area as a region not surpassed in picturesque loveliness. In his poem "Monument Mountain" (1821), he characterized the Berkshires in visual terms, as a place to commune with nature. Viewing nature was for Bryant an affirmation of faith in the divine design.

Bryant's promotion of the Berkshires as a place of perfect balance between man and nature, untainted by industrialization, brought other writers and then artists to the area. By the 1850s, Nathaniel Hawthorne, Oliver Wendell Holmes, and Melville were spending time in the Berkshires and encouraging artists to paint here. Many well-to-do visitors and seasonal residents were inspired by the Berkshires to patronize those artists. Artists and patrons alike looked upon the landscape as a shared spiritual experience, which would inspire one's soul to be close to nature—in other words, to be close to the infinite. Such paintings carried a high moral purpose.

Thomas Cole, who laid the foundation for what emerged as the Hudson River School of painters, was one of the first professional landscape artists to work in the region. In 1833, on his way from the Catskill Mountains, where he lived, to Northampton and Boston, he sketched Pontoosuc Lake, the middle branch of the Housatonic. The painting that followed, entitled *View of Hoosac Mountain and Pontoosuc Lake Near Pittsfield, Massachusetts* (page 18), shows the view north to Saddleball Mountain and Mount Greylock, known at the time as Hoosac Mountain. In it Cole paints nature and civilization in a harmony sanctioned by God (the church steeple of distant Lanesboro) and preserved for the American people, though the tree stump and ax in the lower left signal the relentless advance of civilization.

Frederic Edwin Church, a pupil of Cole's best known for his paintings of the Hudson and exotic locations, came to the Berkshires in 1847 under the patronage of Cyrus W. Field, entrepreneur of the Atlantic telegraph and a native of Stockbridge. Church already had Berkshire connections, as his father and uncle owned a lumber mill in Lee. Church's painting for Field, *View Near Stockbridge,* celebrates the Housatonic as it meanders through the peaceful, pastoral plain of Stockbridge and past the Field property in a quintessential Arcadian scene.

Not all artists averted their eyes from the built environment. Anthon Henry Wenzler exhibited a *View of Great Barrington* in 1849 (at right), a scene looking across fields and the river toward the looming dome of Mount Everett. Wenzler focuses on the fences, boardinghouses, mill structures, church spire, and farmhouses— but he alludes to no tension or disjunction between the civilized landscape and the natural landscape. Rather, he equates the two worlds as harmonious under the same warm sun and takes care that even the church spire is not seen to rise above the hillside. The painting conforms with a general perception of industry in the Berkshires as having reassuringly little presence. Wenzler celebrates the progress of civilization as assured by the balanced relationship among nature, God, and industrious Americans.

Jasper Cropsey used the studio of his friend and fellow painter Charles Gaylord in Gaylordsville, near Kent, and roamed the area in 1845, a visit best recorded in his landscape *Schatacook Mountain, Housatonic Valley, Connecticut,* now in the collection of the Museum of Fine Arts in Boston. He returned to paint Twin Lakes in Salisbury a few years later. Twin Lakes was a favorite destination of

Anthon Henry Wenzler
View of Great Barrington

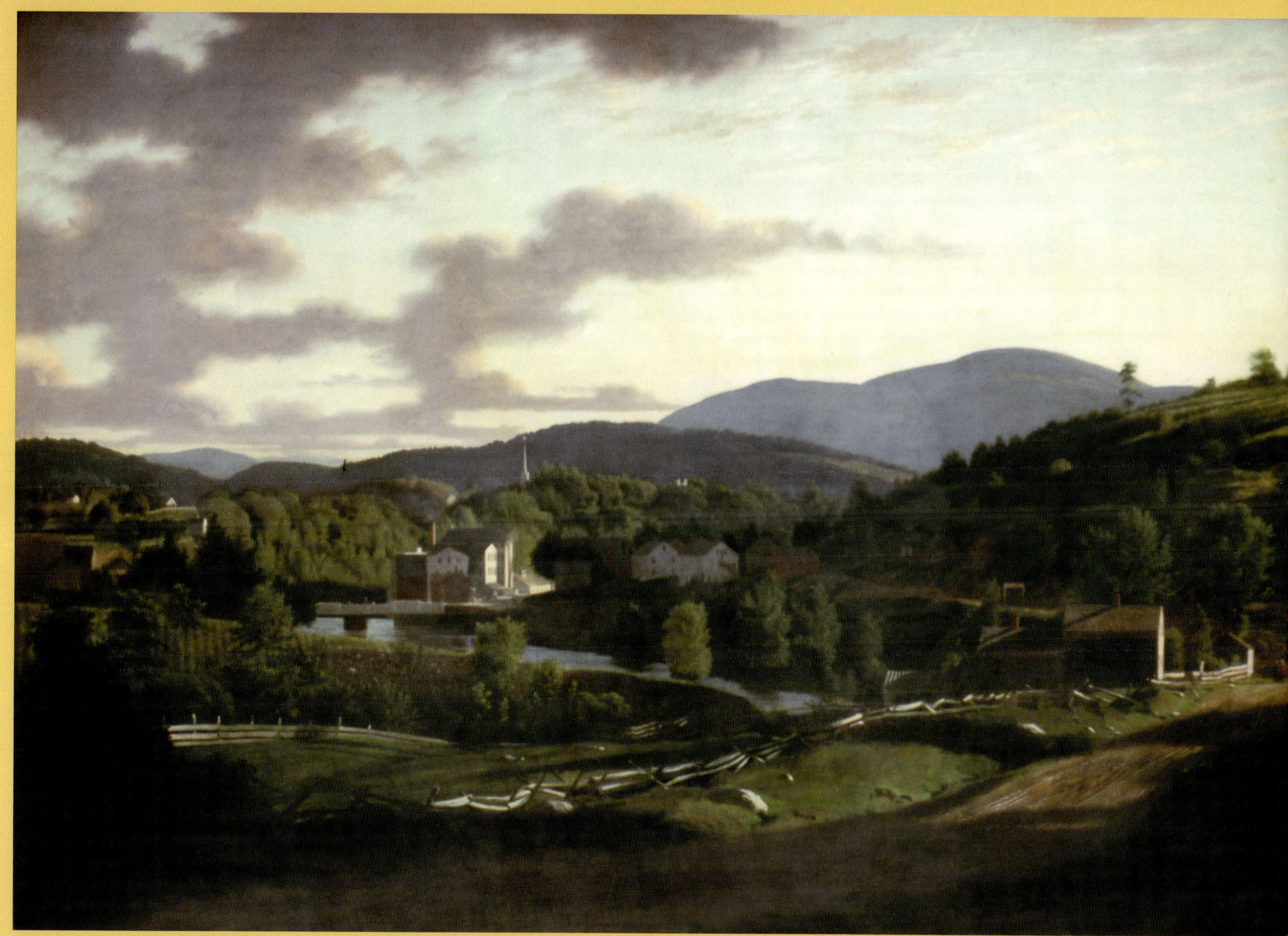

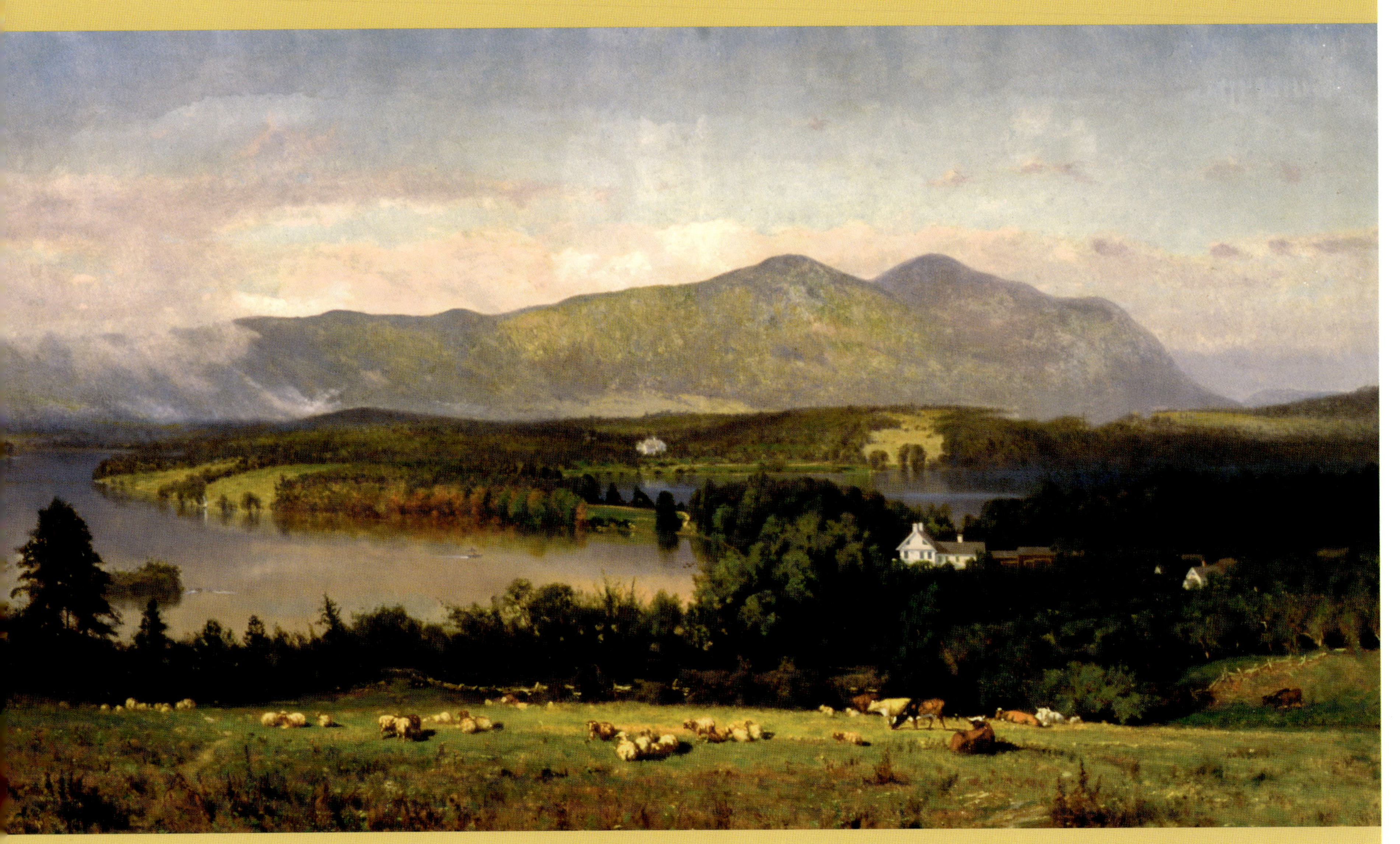

Edward Gay
Twin Lakes with Cattle

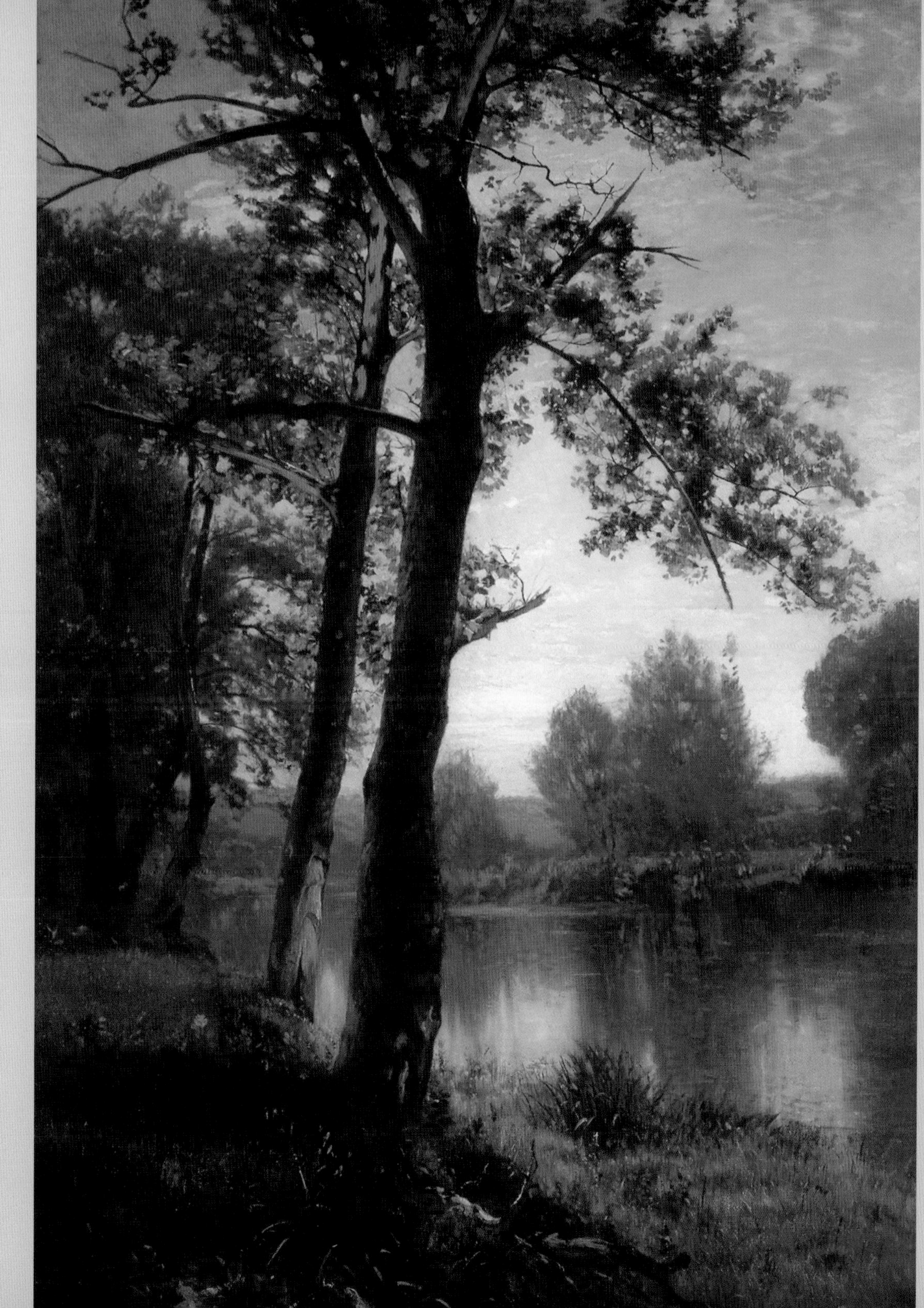

Arthur Parton

Scene on the Housatonic River

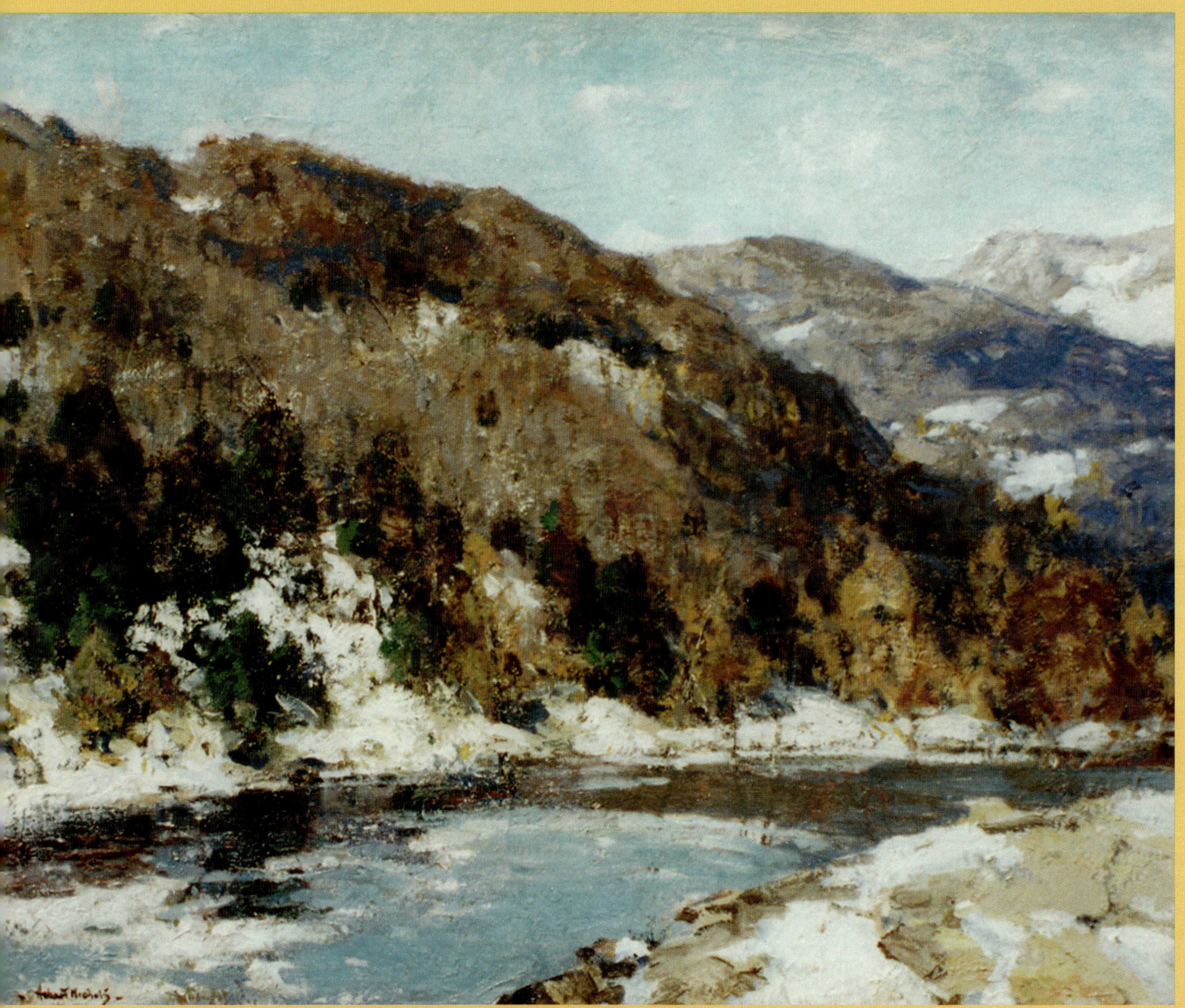

artists in those years, also painted by Homer Dodge Martin, Richard Hubbard, James Renwick Brevoort, Edwin White, and others. Edward Gay painted *Twin Lakes with Cattle* in 1868 (page 22). The painting was commissioned by Frederick Miles, whose house is the white building next to the lake.

Other painters associated with the Hudson River School who painted in the Housatonic region include John Kensett and Sanford Gifford. Asher B. Durand, who succeeded Cole as the leader of the Hudson River School, painted Monument Mountain in the 1850s. His *Scene Among the Berkshire Hills,* 1872, was painted for Walter Wright of Chicago, who described the elements of the Berkshires he wanted to have in this landscape in a letter to the artist: "uncultivated scenes of native mountains, hills, vales, streams, brooks and waterfalls, trees and woods…." Durand executed this commission by painting a vista from the lawn at Tanglewood, including the Housatonic, Stockbridge Bowl, Monument Mountain, and Mount Everett beyond. Durand, who believed that nature was fraught with lessons of high and holy meaning only surpassed by the light of Revelation, had a great influence on other artists in the area.

By the late 1850s, younger artists also received inspiration from the English aesthetic theorist John Ruskin, who made the principle of truth to nature a rallying cry for the next decade. William Stanley Haseltine and Aaron Draper Shattuck presented closely observed scenes in naturalistic terms. Samuel Coleman painted watercolors of meadows near Great Barrington. William Trost Richards painted in Canaan, the last stop in Connecticut on the Housatonic Valley Railroad.

The French Barbizon artists—including Jean-Baptiste-Camille Corot, Pierre-Etienne-Theodore Rousseau, and Jean-Francois Millet—worked primarily in the forested and agrarian areas around the village of Barbizon, outside Paris. By the 1850s they had reordered priorities in landscape painting, rejecting classical formulas in favor of personal impressions made directly from nature. The brushstrokes were loose and the colors captured the mist, sunsets, seasons, and moods of nature. American artists, influenced by the

Hobart Nichols
Housatonic in Winter

Barbizon style and also by tonalism, a style that used a limited palette to express a particular vision or mood, began to stress their own subjective response to describe the physical details of nature.

The most influential American advocate of Barbizon aims and techniques was George Inness, one of the most important artists who painted in the Berkshires. His early paintings, done for patrons Henry Ward Beecher, Ogden Haggerty, and Samuel Gray Ward, were inspired by European masters more than by Hudson River School precepts. By the 1860s he had shifted to a more abstract, subjective style. His pastoral landscapes, such as *In the Berkshires* (1868 or 1869), are peaceful, religious inspirations composed from memory. As Inness reacted on emotional and spiritual levels to remembered impressions, he intensified his colors, loosened his brushwork, and generalized forms such as cows and trees to the point of indistinctness. His later paintings of the Berkshires are very abstract.

David Johnson had earlier painted in New York state and New England. Working in the Litchfield Hills as a mature artist, he often depicted the Housatonic River. His *Scenery on the Housatonic* was in the Paris Salon exhibition in 1877, and the French press proclaimed him the American Rousseau.

Another painter working in the Barbizon style was Arthur Parton. A specialist in rendering streams and rivers, particularly in the Adirondacks and Catskills, Parton's *Scene on the Housatonic* (page 23) probably dates from the 1880s. In this instance he captured a characteristic recollection of summer in the Berkshires, produced entirely in his New York studio. Parton's loose stroke and interest in atmospheric effects can be attributed to his admiration for Corot and other Barbizon artists. The composition, diffused light, and tonal harmony add to a scene of peace and contentment.

Ben Foster, who had worked in Barbizon, brought the style to Cornwall, Connecticut, in 1893 or 1894, late in his career. A small group that formed around his studio in the Cream Hill section of Cornwall became known as the Cream Hill Group. Alexander T. Van Laer worked in Litchfield around the same time, his palette lightening as the years went on so that his later landscapes came closer to the high-key colors of impressionism.

By the end of the 1800s, the influence of the French Impressionists was spreading in America. Connecticut by then had several art colonies—at Silvermine, Mystic, Cos Cob, Old Lyme. The colony at Falls Village/Lime Rock, close to scenic subjects such as the covered bridge at Cornwall and the Great Falls of the Housatonic, sprang up in 1910 around Emil Carlsen, Willard Leroy Metcalf, Robert Reid, William Carrigan, and other painters.

The colony at Kent coalesced at the same time around artists such as Robert Nisbet, Willard Paddock, Francis Mora, Frederick Waugh, and Spencer Baird Nichols. They painted scenes of the Berkshires and the Connecticut hills and exhibited in both the Kent Art Association and the Stockbridge Art Association. Hobart Nichols, a regular visitor of his brother Spencer, often painted with the group around Kent and in the Berkshires, especially scenes of snow. He loved the physical act of painting and practiced a vigorous form of impressionism, with long, dashing brushstrokes. Painted in 1925, *Housatonic in Winter* (page 24) shows his flat, impressionistic style, with thick pigment and brush marks.

While an art colony along the lines of those in Kent and Falls Village never sprang up in Stockbridge, that town had the Stockbridge Art Association. It held annual shows from 1909 to 1933 that attracted many of the Connecticut painters, along with artists working in Berkshire County and New York City.

Joseph Jefferson, Thomas Craig, Hugh Bolton Jones, and his wife, Olive Parker Black, all well-known Barbizon painters attracted to impressionism, lived and worked in the Berkshires at this time. From the 1890s to the 1920s, Jones and Black vacationed annually at a rented cottage in South Egremont, where they painted soft and idyllic scenes of the river and the Berkshire Hills.

The American artists of the nineteenth and early twentieth centuries preserved for society a cultural perspective on the landscape that still prevails today. Beyond the occasional cloudy sky or vigorous gesture of brushstroke, there is no hint of strife in these pastoral scenes. The Berkshires and Litchfield Hills are still regarded as a sanctuary from stress, materialism, and other worldly cares for many who seek peace and solitude in their idyllic hills, rivers, and fields. The Housatonic River, still mighty, brings beauty and music to each hamlet it runs through as it quietly reflects the Berkshires and the Litchfield Hills. As William Cullen Bryant said more than 100 years ago:

> The woods were in all the glory of autumn, and I well remember, as I passed through Stockbridge, how much I was struck by the beauty of the smooth, green meadows, on the banks of that lovely river…the Housatonic, and whose gently flowing waters seemed tinged with the gold and crimson of the trees that overhung them. I admired no less the contrast between this soft scene and the steep, craggy hills that overlooked it, clothed with their many colored forests.

RECENT READINGS OF THE HOUSATONIC

Geoffrey Young

Geoffrey Young moved to the Berkshires from Berkeley in 1982. "Lights Out," a book of his poems with drawings by James Siena, came out in 2003. For the past 13 summers he has directed the Geoffrey Young Gallery in Great Barrington.

Sometimes it takes a dog. One sunny cold morning while walking our toothless dog up Castle Hill Avenue I first saw white clouds of steam rising from the Housatonic River as it flowed, unseen below, through Great Barrington.

At once I was reminded that we too are a kind of river civilization–like Paris, London, Rome, or Budapest. As water encourages settlement, and settlement commerce, traffic requires bridges, and bridges afford views of the water coming toward you, the water flowing by.

The desire to make something of these sweeping views has ever been a part of art's ambition. Leonardo's Madonna and St. Anne sit in a grotto with the water of life flowing nearby. The Romantics and Impressionists never saw a body of water that didn't heighten their feelings or break up light in perfect answer to aesthetic needs.

Today's painters inherit the strands of several rich traditions of artistic response to the river, starting with the Hudson River School. Even pioneer abstractionist Arshile Gorky used the Housatonic and surrounding countryside as springboards toward innovation, while living in Sherman, Connecticut, in the 1940s.

Now, at the dawn of a new millennium, many centuries into the history of easel painting, the meandering lines and smeared light on the Housatonic still exert their powerful influences on contemporary artists. Just as Egyptian civilization would never have existed without Nile River water, it is doubtful we'd be living here in a succession of small Berkshire and Litchfield towns without the Housatonic's scenic presence.

If you've ever cooled off in the Green River on a scorching summer afternoon, you might feel, as I do, that this tributary to the Housatonic is a sacred place, sacred in the way that Greeks gave godly status to certain streams, rivers, and limestone caverns, tying their spirit stories to the power and beauty of place.

Shall we gather at the river? Painters position themselves to see what's coming, what's going, to check out the water under the bridge. As Twain studied the Mississippi and Thoreau the Concord and the Merrimack, we have the Housatonic River. Southward the river moves, rippling over low rocks, speeding through narrows, making wide slow turns, a marvel with a checkered history, on the slow rebound after having suffered years of environmental distress.

Artists who take a measure of their inspiration from the river strive to capture the lingering atmospheric light that mirrors the shoreline's vegetation, the kind of thing we might see from a passing car window, or while hiking, or from the bow of a canoe moving quietly. We reach for our

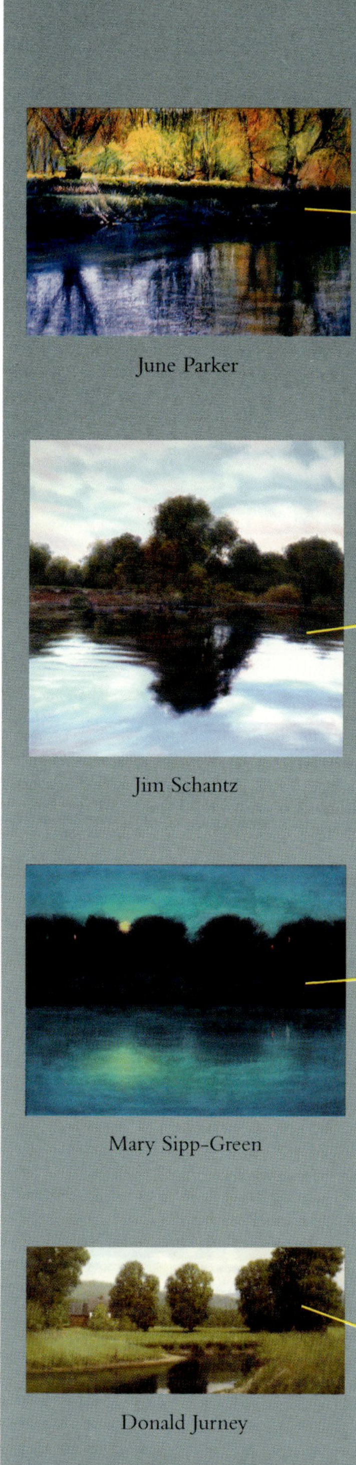

June Parker

Jim Schantz

Mary Sipp-Green

Donald Jurney

camera to preserve the shimmering reflection of trees in water, knowing that the fleeting Edenic moment soon passes when light and the things it hits are at their maximum saturation. June Parker's *Riverbank* (page 33) shows October's bright yellows and oranges undergoing a cooling transformation as their autumnal fire is inverted on the water's surface, breaking up, wobbling, the blue pastel of her water registering perfectly the season's fall toward winter, as if extinguishing the brightness in the inevitable chill of shadow.

Jim Schantz puts the reflection of a clump of trees in the center of *September, Housatonic Reflection* (page 34), then surrounds its lavender-tinged mystery with high, lazy summer clouds and airy blue sky, suggesting great distances, timeless expanses, calling into question the exact location of any surface. The ambiguous nature of Schantz's water invites meditation on the temporal and the eternal. On process and reality. The surface swells with its own illusory presence.

Whether high in the evening sky, or rising behind an embankment of trees, the moon in Mary Sipp-Green's *River Lights* (page 35) sheds its diffuse light upon the water, coloring the mood with enchantment, as if there were ample opportunity to "loafe and invite your soul" into this atmospheric moment. The saturated darks of the silhouetted trees on the far shore of the river admit but little light, the sky flowing overhead, the water pooling with light below. The warm moonlight peeking between the space of two trees hits the water and diminishes the reflection of the very trees it is rising over. This water can take us to Shangri-la, and we don't even need a ticket.

Sometimes an otherwise insignificant detail grabs attention, as in Donald Jurney's wide-angled view of a stream, *South County Summer* (page 36).

A single post by the water's edge stands there, squat, reflected in the all but still water, asking nothing of us. While the rest of the picture provides atmosphere and expanse—acres of green grasses and fully dressed trees, through which we know the river is flowing, however languidly—this post, which could be a stump of a tree, reminds us of nothing so much as the agency of the artist in charge of the composition, a sly reference to creative autonomy.

If the river views of Schantz, Parker, Sipp-Green, and Jurney seem timeless, Warner Friedman's *Free Ride to the Housatonic* (page 37) introduces a contemporary element. His way of claiming the picture for our time is to present his view of the river as if seen on the other side of a rigorous sculpture in 3D (a primary structure by Sol LeWitt, Tony Smith, or Robert Morris, say). And the pleasure we get is twofold: one, the restful view feels accurate, unharried (the shadows in nature are as darkly saturated as the unilluminated side of the sculpture); and two, the view's shape, a parallelogram rather than a rectangle, is dictated by the geometric angles of the primary structure, Friedman's eccentric polygon. The hard-edged object, carefully toned in various grays and black, is no less important to the painting and to Friedman's art, than conventional notions about beauty in nature. His painting unites two otherwise opposite strains in American art: minimalist abstraction and traditional landscape, valorizing both.

Earlier painters had used the river as a way to move toward abstraction. In 1932, freshly back from study with Fernand Léger in Paris, George L. K. Morris painted *Housatonic River* (page 38) and other Berkshire scenes in an idealized style much indebted to the proto-cubist watercolors of Paul Cézanne. In *Housatonic River,* two male bathers relax at the

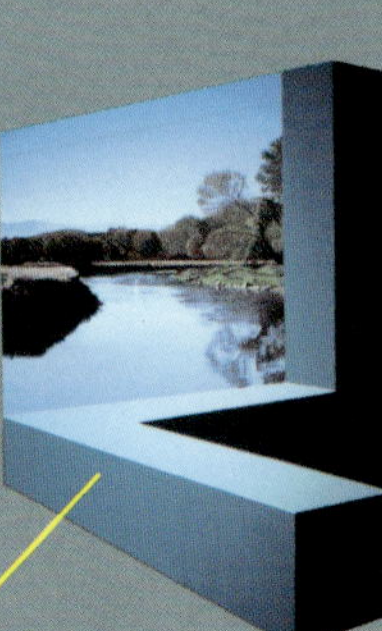

Warner Friedman

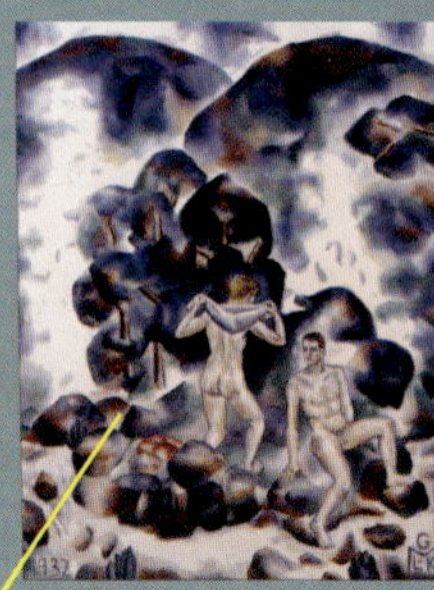

George L. K. Morris

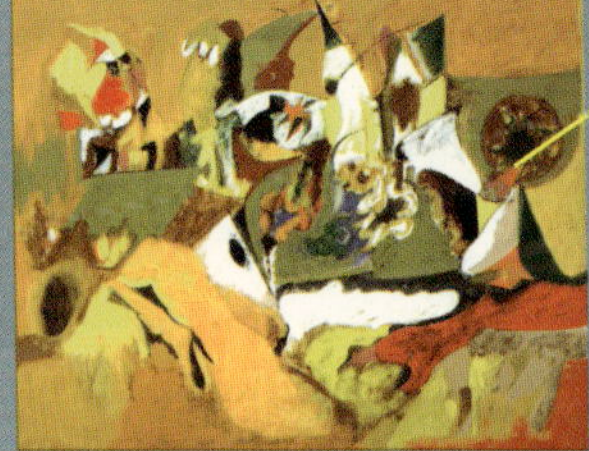

Arshile Gorky

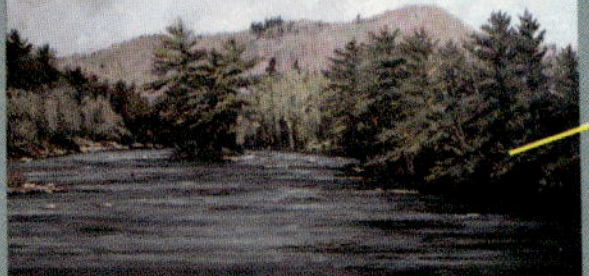

Emily Buchanan

water's edge, one toweling off, the other seated with a foot touching the water. The white rush of water (like the mist in the air) seems to be cascading down past their nude bodies. They have been swimming or wading, something easily and perhaps fearlessly done back before the river was polluted. The cloud-like mountains, the stylized trees, and the carefully modeled figures give this scene a unified feeling of theatrical purity, of a peaceable kingdom made stylish and elegant by the artist's technically adventurous conception. Within a few short years of this work, Morris would devote himself exclusively to American Abstractionism.

Gorky's autumnally toned *Golden Brown,* from 1943-44 (page 39), is dense with incident, which includes half-buried figurative elements and, according to one scholar, a dancer's shape bending back and blending into the landscape. Though an exact description of the elements may be impossible to state, his drawing and color suggest movement, as of water flowing around rocks or over falls, his way of giving body to objects in the landscape leading him very close to pure abstraction.

For sport, besides hiking and canoeing, the river offers fishermen the chance to bait up and cast into the current—and they come from around the world to partake. Emily Buchanan's *Spring Along the Housatonic* (page 40) captures one such fly fisherman whose red shirt stands out against the gorgeous striations of the gray-blue rippling water whose width fills the bottom of her picture, as if seen through a wide-angled lens. We can see through Buchanan's shallow, transparent paint to the rock-strewn bottom, imagine the pressure of the current on the body of the fisherman, admire the authentic tilt of the trees as their boughs sough shadows at the river's edge. The horizontal modulation of her various shades of blue paint as the rocky bottom bumps the water along reminds us to look longer if we want to see what movement looks like. Spring will arrive, but the trees on the distant hill have not leafed out yet.

As seen from the vantage of a shoreline boulder or bridge, John Manikowski shows a part of the river in *River Pool with Trout* (page 41) where dark water flowing over a drop-off turns bubbly white, with autumn leaves gathering in the spaces between boulders that line the water's edge. Perhaps no longer edible, but there to show us what lives in the water, toward which fishermen still cast their lines, is a speckled trout, a species and an individual, isolated for our visual benefit. When will trout from the Housatonic be edible again?

Years ago I was the token writer amidst a handful of artists in South County (as Berkshire County below Stockbridge is known) who met in a life-drawing class and later formed a group called the Cornball Club. Each year we awarded the Cornball Trophy to one of our members who exemplified by his or her activity an essential understanding of the cornball concept (not that I can remember with any precision what that concept was). After a number of years went by, and each of us had been awarded this obscurely prestigious award (each winner's name was added to the trophy, said trophy being topped with a paintbrush), we realized we had to dissolve the club, since it had performed its role by making winners of us all.

After our last supper, we took the trophy, which was now attached to a model wooden boat made by Morgan Bulkeley, Jr. (son of writer and naturalist Morgan Bulkeley) down to the

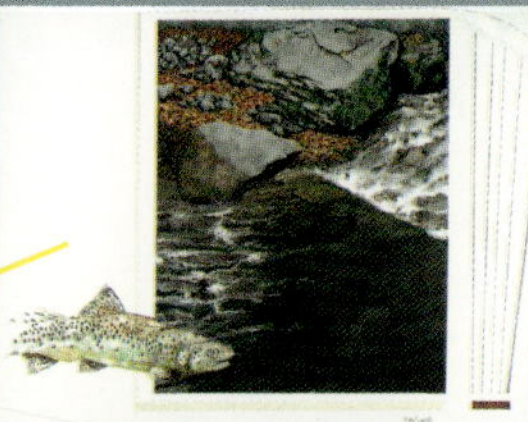

John Manikowski

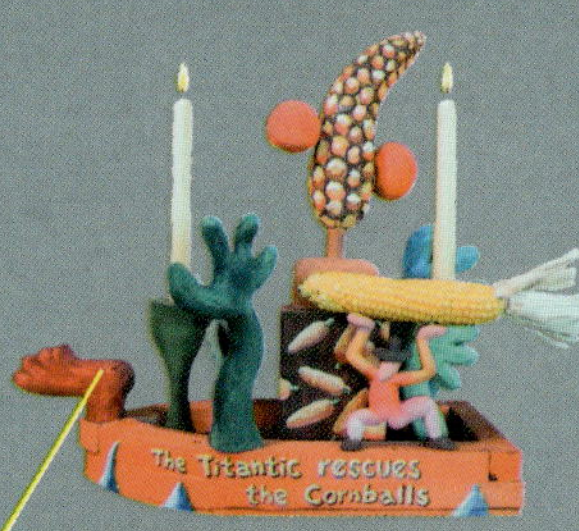

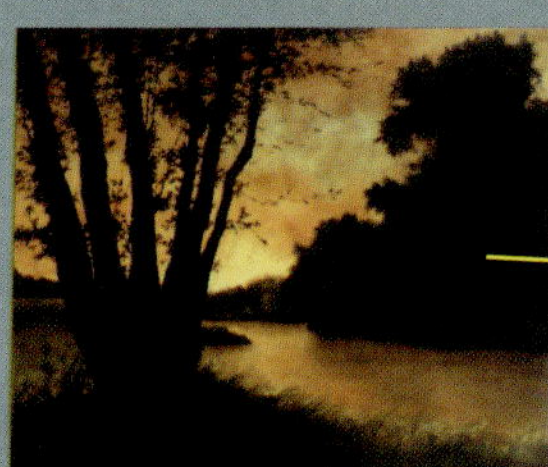

Gabrielle Senza

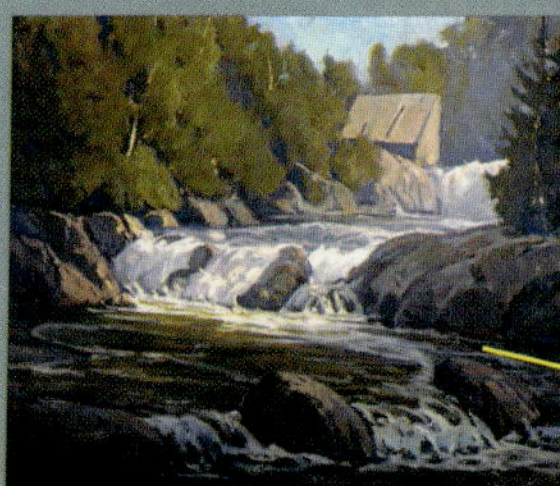

Helen Nichols Jacobs

Housatonic River behind Don Jurney's and Joan Griswold's house. After singing many songs in the dark, we lit the candles attached to the boat and set it flowing downstream, the trophy with our names proudly displayed being carried in the current toward some fate unknown. Would the vessel sink, or would someone find the boat four towns downstream and give us a call? Or would the candles ignite deadwood at the water's edge and cause a conflagration? We toasted its chances of survival and returned to the house, exhilarated but exhausted from the bibulous proceedings, our group mythically disbanded, our shoes caked with mud.

I mention this story because the Housatonic River gives it a dimension it might otherwise have lacked, by doing what rivers do: flow downstream, taking anything that floats with them. To float downstream has ever been a high achievement. As our little boat rounded the bend, and slowly left our sight, its flickering candles still burning, never to be seen again, we were history.

Gabrielle Senza's paintings are history of another kind. Her vegetation-lined river, *Il Silencio di Luce VII* (page 42), bathed in ancient light—a light whose glow seems to trigger the memory of timeless idylls—is caught in that between-time as day becomes dusk, her many-trunked tree in the foreground like a sentinel taking it all in, while being part of it. Not a time to swim, boat, or even ford the river: Senza's light invites reverie. We can feel our shoes dampen in the dew of her shoreline grasses as we experience the evening's brief but amazing last burst of illumination.

Kent native Helen Nichols Jacobs gets the tumbling, swirling feel of the Housatonic in her *Rushing Water at Bulls Bridge* (page 43). Jacobs, niece of Hobart Nichols, whose work is in this book's historic section, paints the water pouring white over the falls in the upper right, and moves laterally and down through the picture until it trickles away from a moss-green pool, safely on its way. Pinpricks of light fleck vegetation and rock, dot white water and blue, capturing a certain slant of sunlight in the rhythm of the water's descent.

How many different ways there are to see and capture the look of flowing water. The same phenomenon that got Leonardo's attention (his studies of moving water are seminal) continues to attract contemporary artists. Erica Child Prud'homme's *Under the Bridge: Spring Melt* (page 44) is a wide-angled look at the nearly patterned folds that water makes as it presses against and is diverted by the stanchion of a bridge. Like brain coral, or the folds in epoxied cloth, the mysteriously organic look of her water is both convincingly wet and utterly abstract, a stop-frame analysis of what never stops changing. In its surge, and chill, we get an inkling of the power and otherness of nature.

The river has its problems, and one of them is suggested by Geoffrey Moss, who has been painting the Housatonic for 23 years. In *Three Beakers* (page 45), a painting from the Water Science series, Moss draws attention to what he calls "a curious embalming" as he reconstructs the vulnerability of an American landscape. In this still life, human intrusion is suggested by the red table, the three beakers, and the rubber tubing that snakes out of the beakers. Though the science of the situation is not precisely known to the viewer, some experiment is going on. Three trees with lavender trunks stand behind the table, clearly part of a larger landscape, while below the table, as if the reflection of a sky, is what looks to

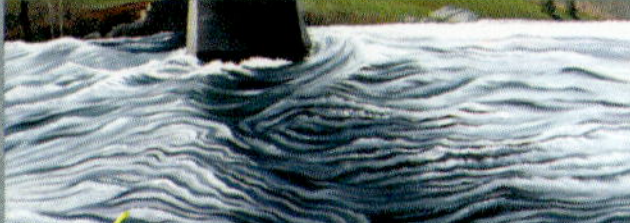

Erica Child Prud'homme

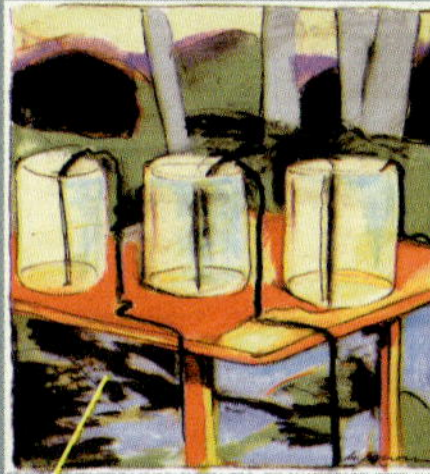

Geoffrey Moss

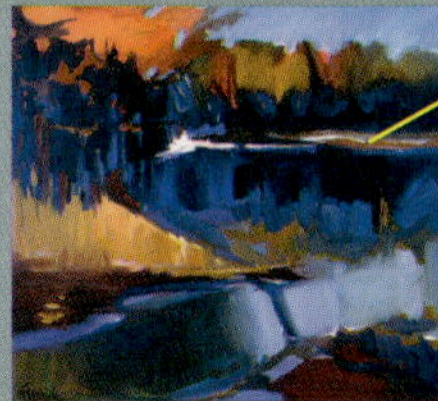

Frank Federico

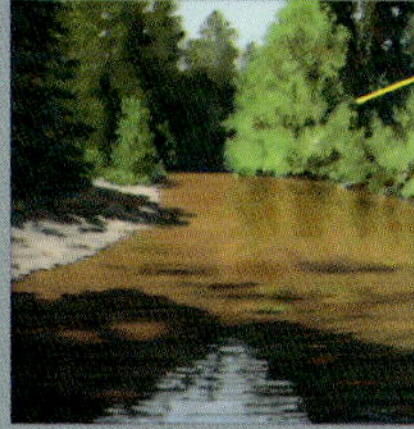

David McCandless

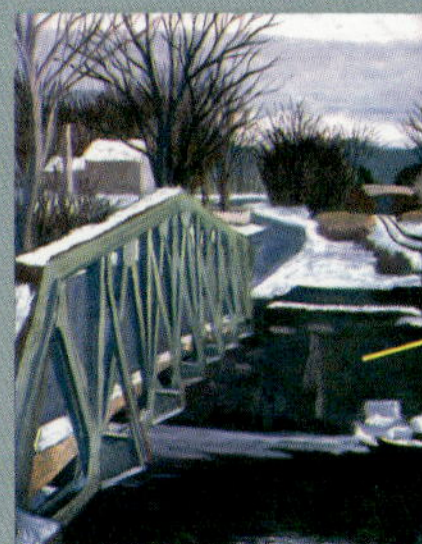

Margot Trout

be the blue of water. If we can't know exactly what is being studied, we can at least hope that testing will continue to monitor water quality as well as flora and fauna health along the river's course.

With expressionistic verve, Frank Federico applies thick, bold brushstrokes in *River Bend* (page 46), careful to register the limousine navy shadows in the pooling water, and with enough agitation to show the force of the river's descent over a slight falls. Autumnal, but not dying, these blocks and spears of color/form balance the competing claims of art and nature, giving primacy to neither, seeming to leap up from the surface or shoot down from the trees, resolving themselves as representation and autonomous aesthetic event, simultaneously.

If Federico's water is rich in shades of blue and violet, Great Barrington native David McCandless's *Housatonic Near Glendale* (page 47) paints the flow of the river in copper tones of lazy afternoon light. How cold is that deceptively warm color? Anyone who has been in the Green River swimming hole along Route 23 knows that color, and is well aware of the penetrating chill of the water. McCandless catches his stretch of the river as it emerges from shadow and returns to shadow, suddenly sun-baked and shallow, keeping his realist's eye on the celebratory warmth of a summer day.

Something there is that loves a bridge. Margot Trout's winter scene, *Green Bridge* (page 48), reveals the water—partially frozen, dark, uninviting—as it moves through the narrowing space below a bridge. The bridge is all X-braced support; the road winds its way out of the picture, through a landscape dusted with snow. In Trout's picture, the impact of our engineering upon the landscape is matter of fact: a bridge takes us where we need to go, safely, and is a structure worthy of our attention in itself. In Ann Getsinger's *Woman, River, and Bridge* (page 49), the bridge functions more as a backdrop to the private (because clothesless) figure seated on sand by the water's edge. Though bathed in afternoon light, this figure could belong to a mythic past. Not a water nymph, but the fecund principle of nature itself, our goddess (communing and vulnerable) might just be missed by any travelers speeding over the bridge.

Son of an engineer, Woldemar Neufeld depicted all 65 bridges crossing the Housatonic River in Connecticut and Massachusetts as a bicentennial project. In *Housatonic Bridge at Kent* (page 50), the scraggly calligraphy of corn stalks in the foreground lead the eye to the dark water's edge and to the view across the river of Kent School's solid institutional brick buildings. The bridge (which is no longer there, I'm told) strikes a bold line across the painting (and the river) and, together with the curving branches of the trees at the water's edge, makes the upper third of the painting a tangle of wandering organic forms and rigorous geometric steel vectors. Agriculture, education, and engineering all meet in a harmony of evenly felt documentary light, at the center of which, and pulling hard, is a crew sculling under the bridge.

To preserve the momentary feeling of an otherwise overlooked scene is one of painting's sterling capacities. Bart Elsbach's *Housatonic Bend from Kellogg Road* (page 51) captures tree reflections on the all but still pool in the foreground, then watches the pool of water reduce in width as it slips past a sandbar only to stop at the midpoint of the painting, a narrow smear of light literally contained (because surrounded) by the density of trees that line the shores. Elsbach's leaves are minute flecks and daubs, his atmosphere is humid. What rings true is

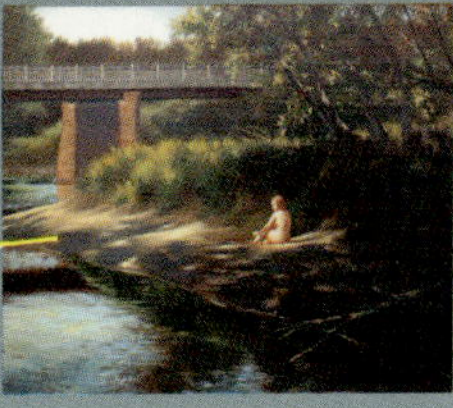

Ann Getsinger

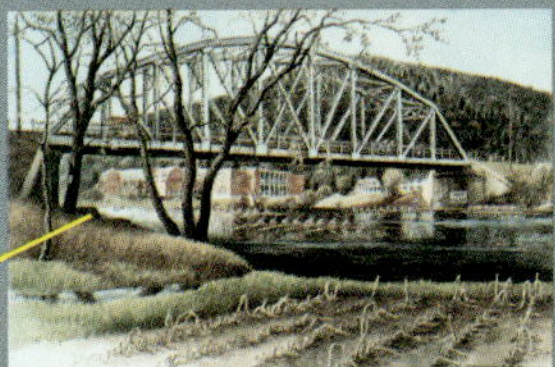

Woldemar Neufeld

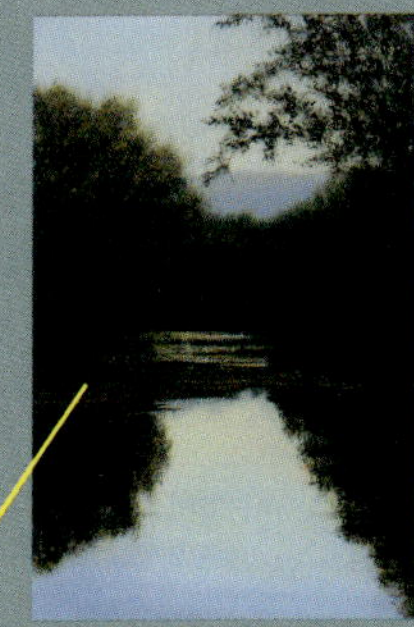

Bart Elsbach

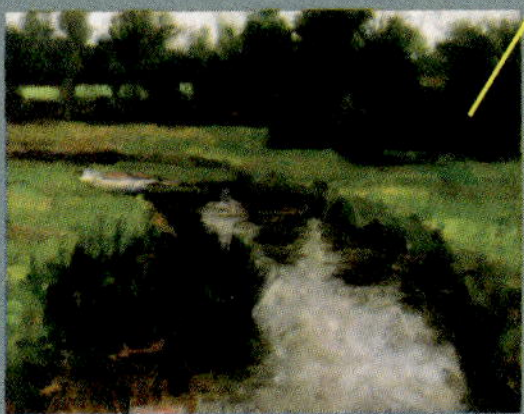

Joan Griswold

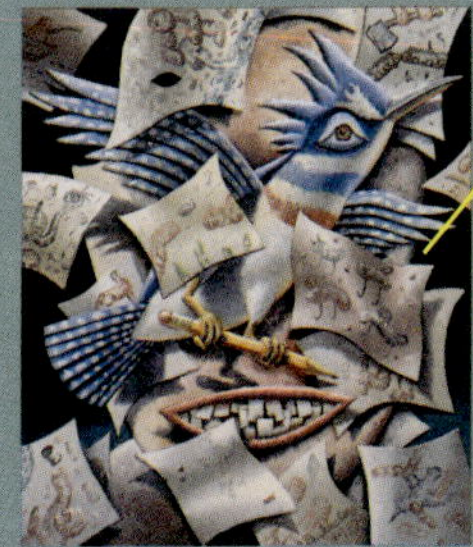

Morgan Bulkeley, Jr.

the serenity of the pool as it mirrors the sky, an unruffled, unknowable depth perfectly observed.

Does anyone know how many tributaries feed the Housatonic?

Joan Griswold's *A Lazy River* (page 52) derives from a stream in Great Barrington near Simon's Rock College, one of many that feed the Housatonic. Her vivid brushstrokes and careful tonal modulations show green to be a color with endless variety. The setting is summer, the mood unhurried, the water will find its way along its bed. Mottled light, reflected on the water, suggests an overcast sky or dense humidity. The eye is attracted to a meadow in the upper left, seen through widely spaced trees, as if on your walk you were going there.

In Morgan Bulkeley, Jr.'s *Kingfisher Sketches* (page 53), a belted kingfisher, partially obscured by what seem to be tiny sheets of paper, is gripping a pencil, as if the pencil were its perch. The implication is these sheets have been drawn on by the bird, each image confessing some crime against the river. Bulkeley's conceit is that he can show what he imagines the kingfisher's complaints might be, whether toxic dumping, logging, or aggressive fishing, as the bird finds its own habitat compromised by the careless presence of man. Each element of the painting is in low relief, having been carved into a hard maple panel. It is as if this kingfisher's narrative, superimposed on the outline of a human head, is being dreamt by the very head it almost wholly obscures. Bulkeley's feeling is that the water, the bird, and human presence are one interconnected ecological knot, but that only human agency can correct human mistakes. If it takes a bird to remind us, so be it.

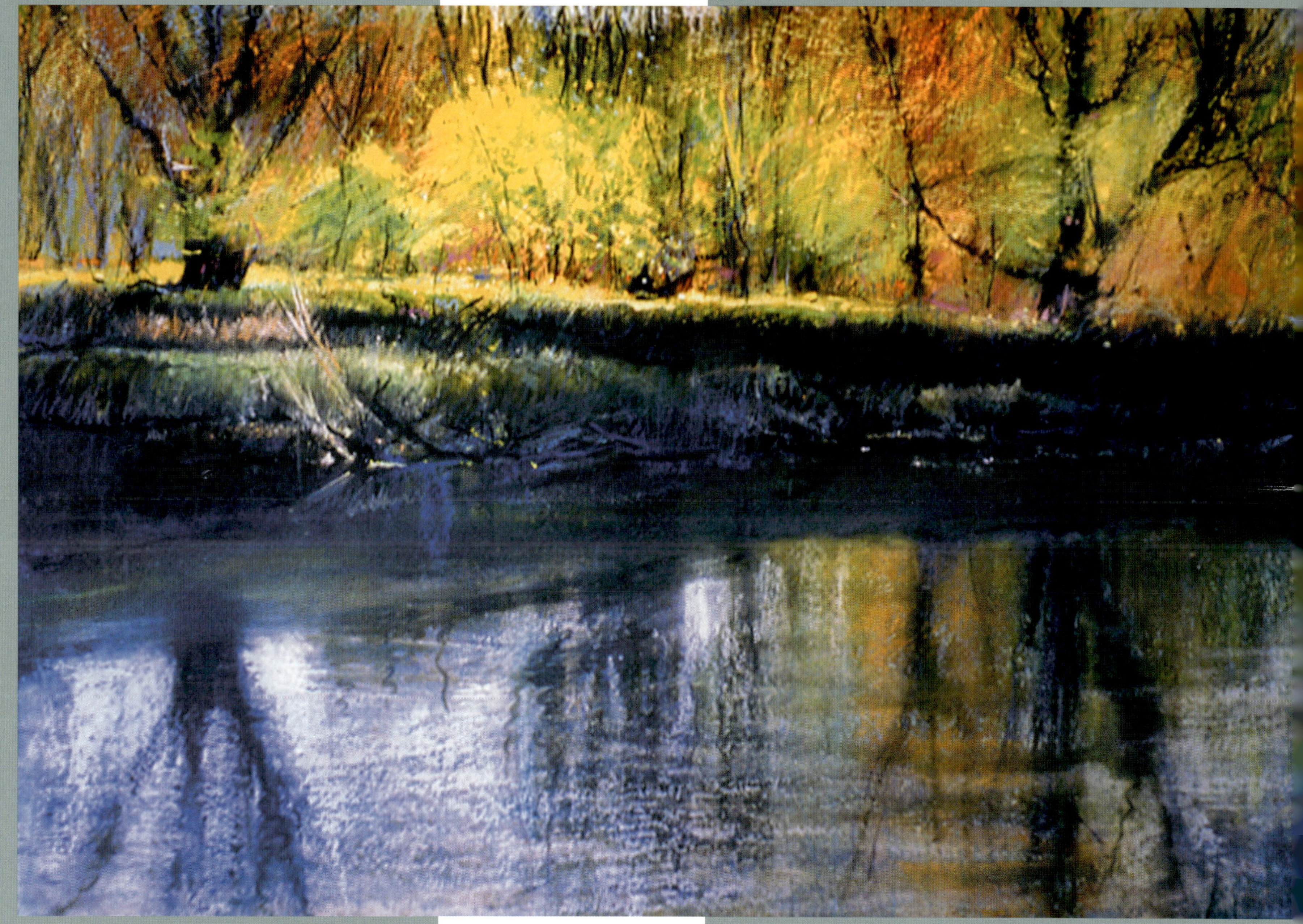

June Parker · *Riverbank*

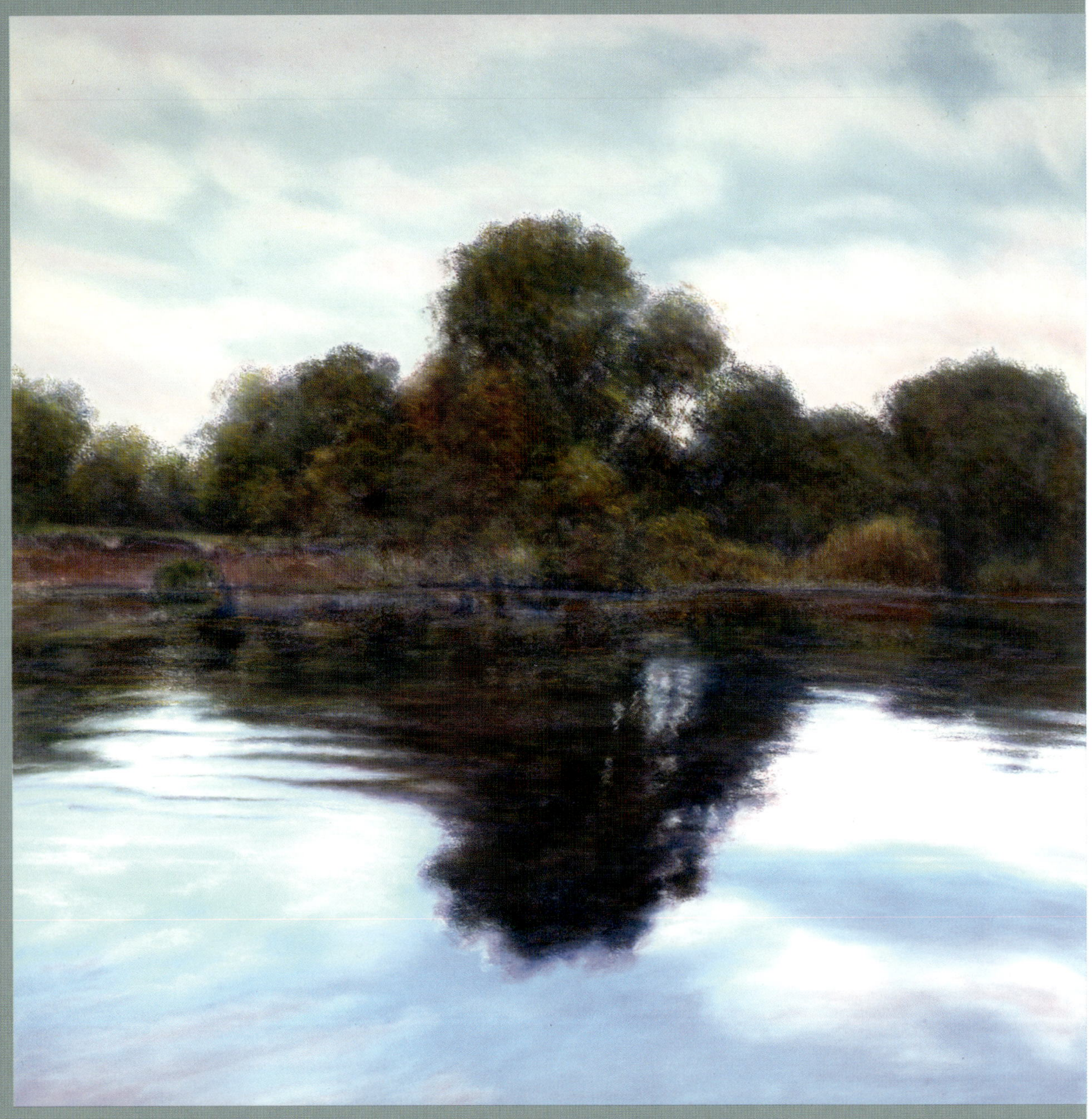

Jim Schantz   *September, Housatonic Reflection*

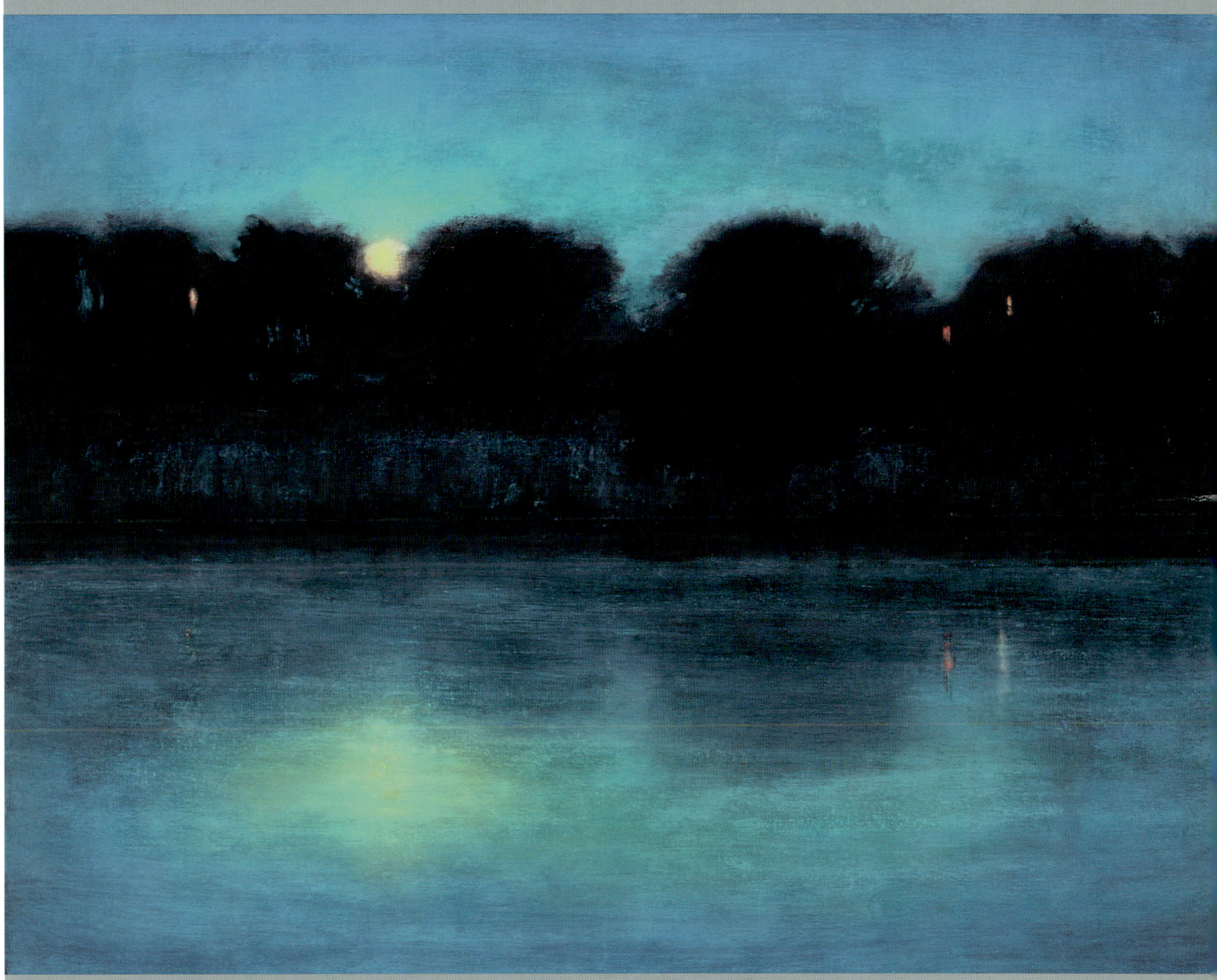

Mary Sipp-Green *River Lights*

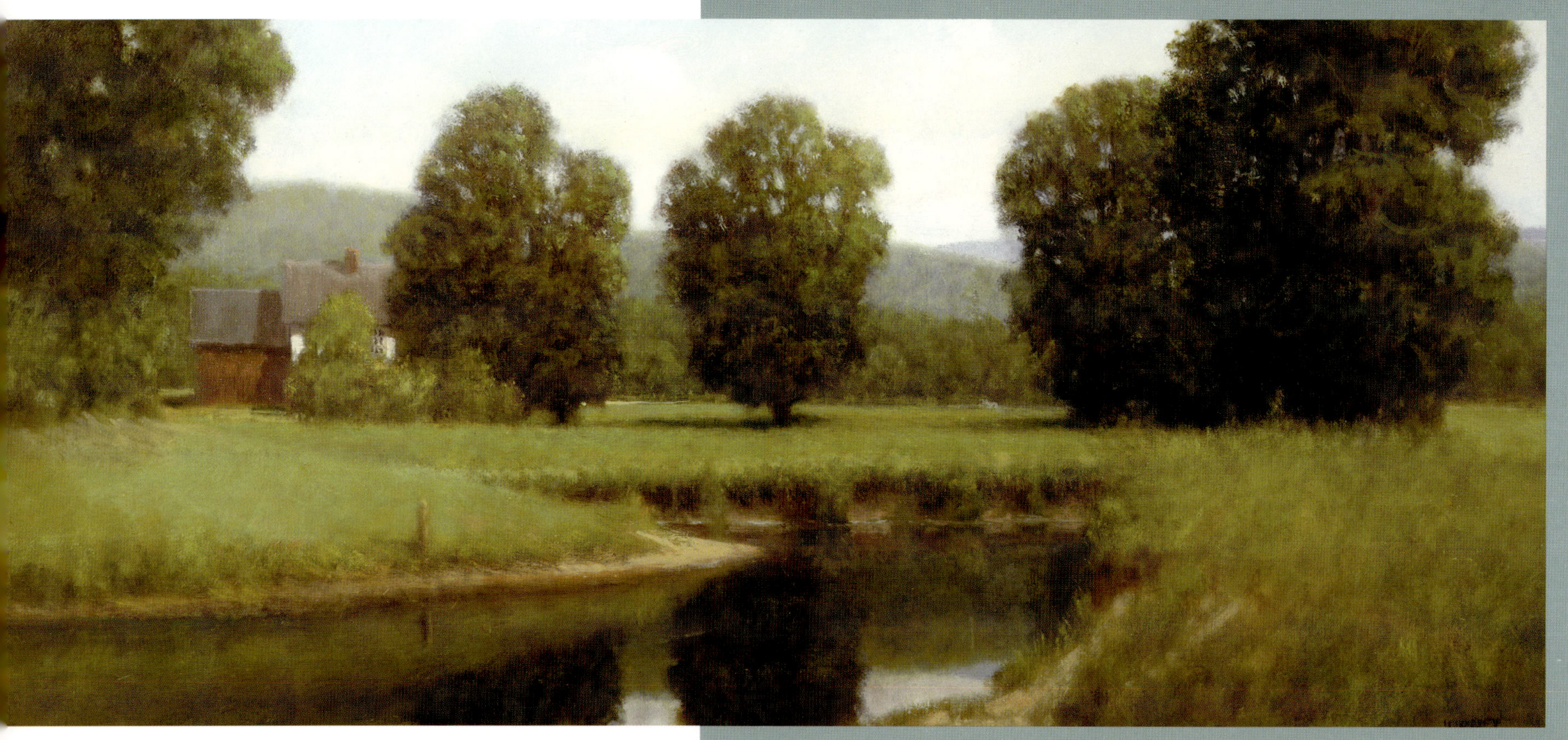

Donald Jurney *South County Summer*

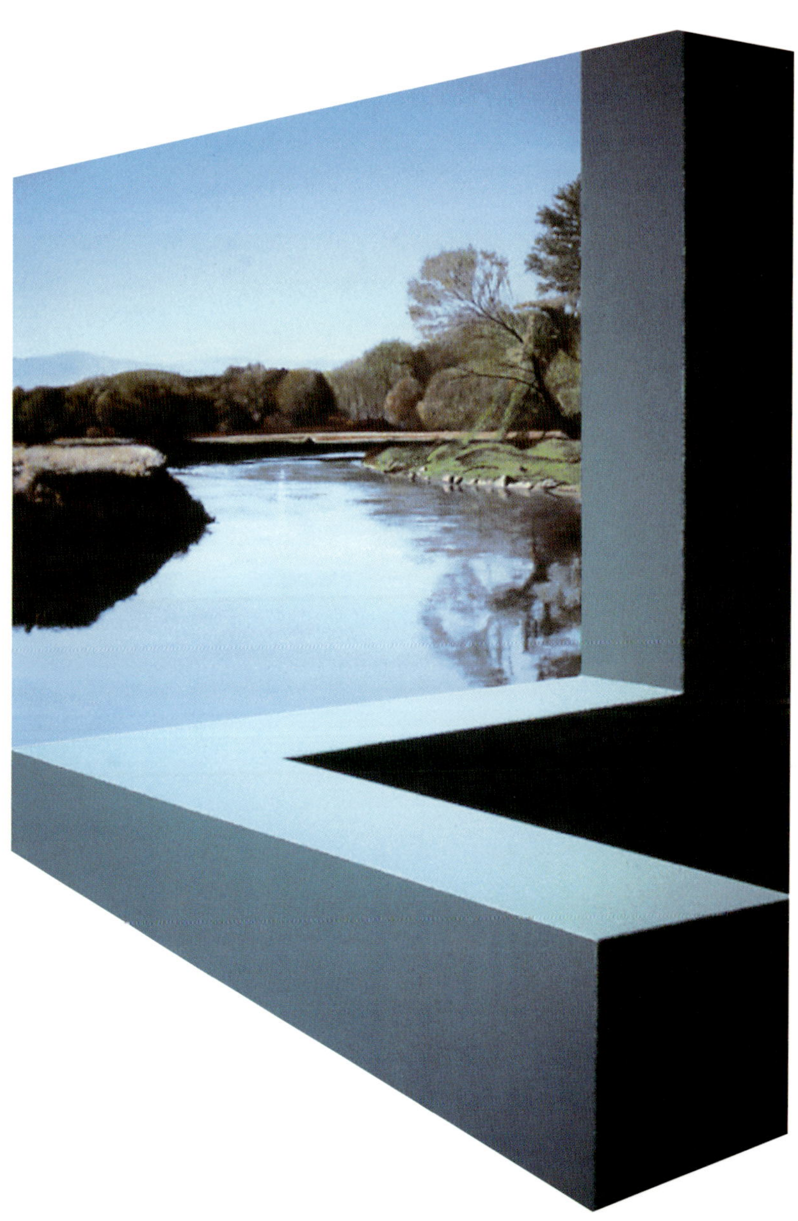

Warner Friedman *Free Ride to the Housatonic*

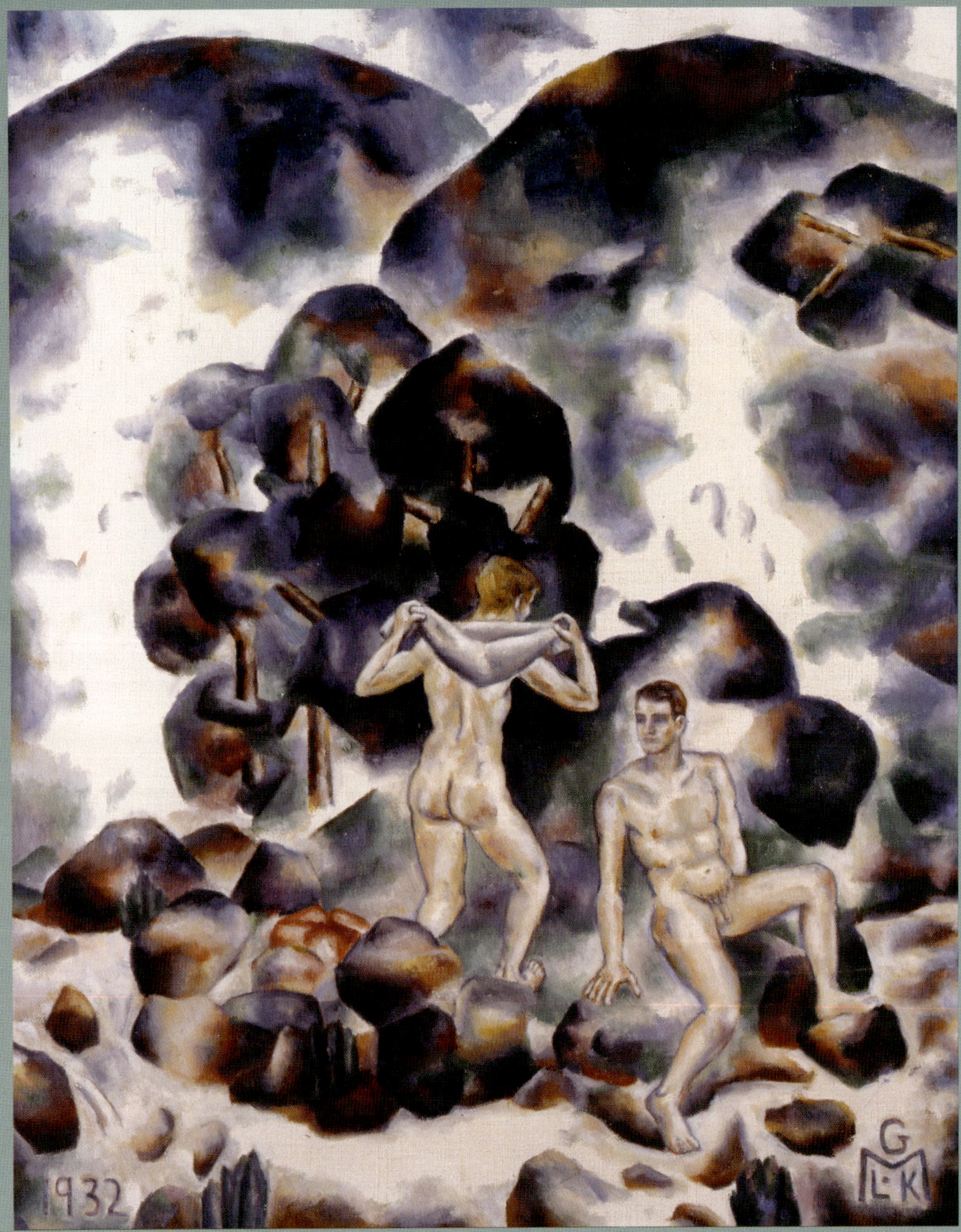

George L. K. Morris *Housatonic River*

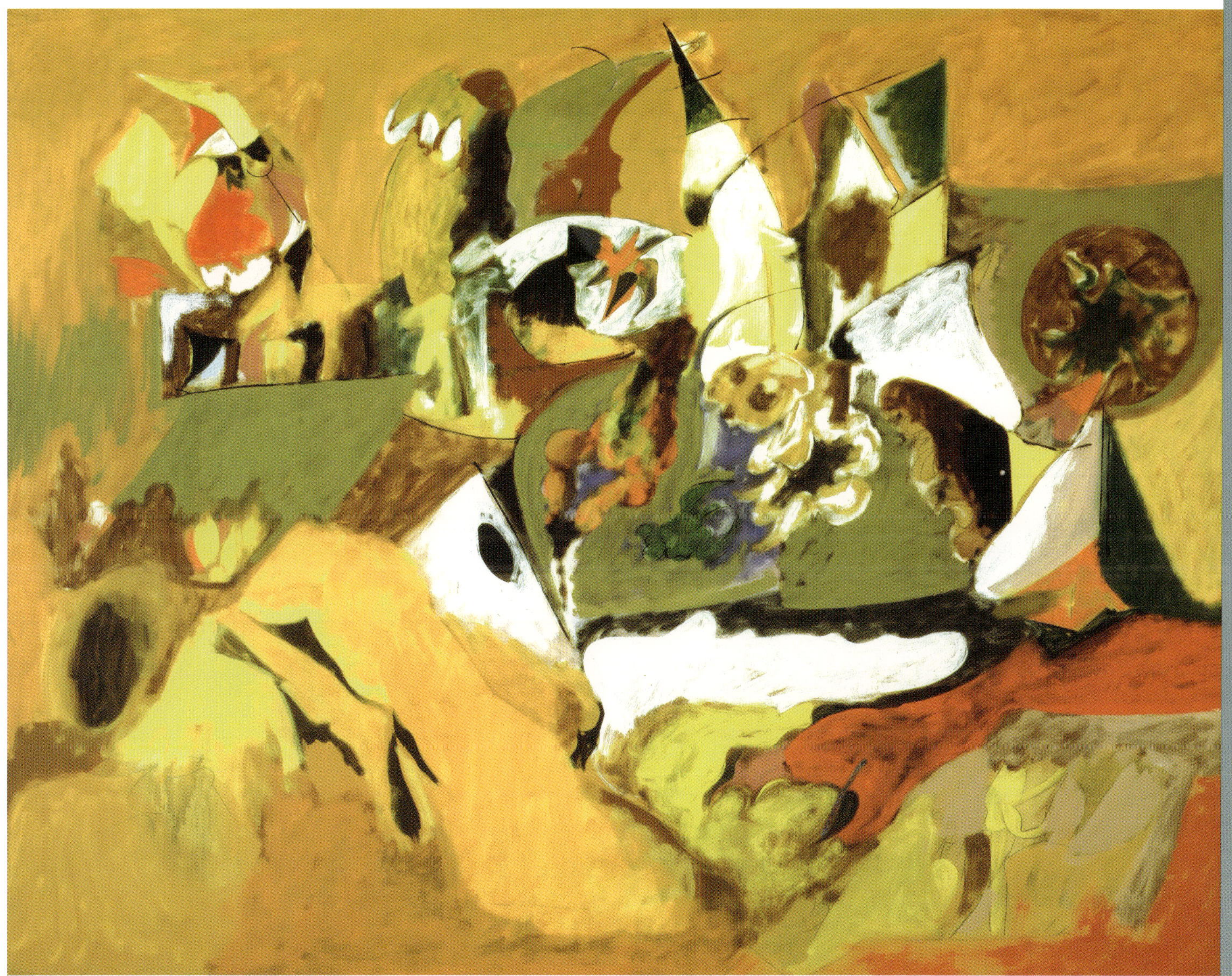

Arshile Gorky *Golden Brown*

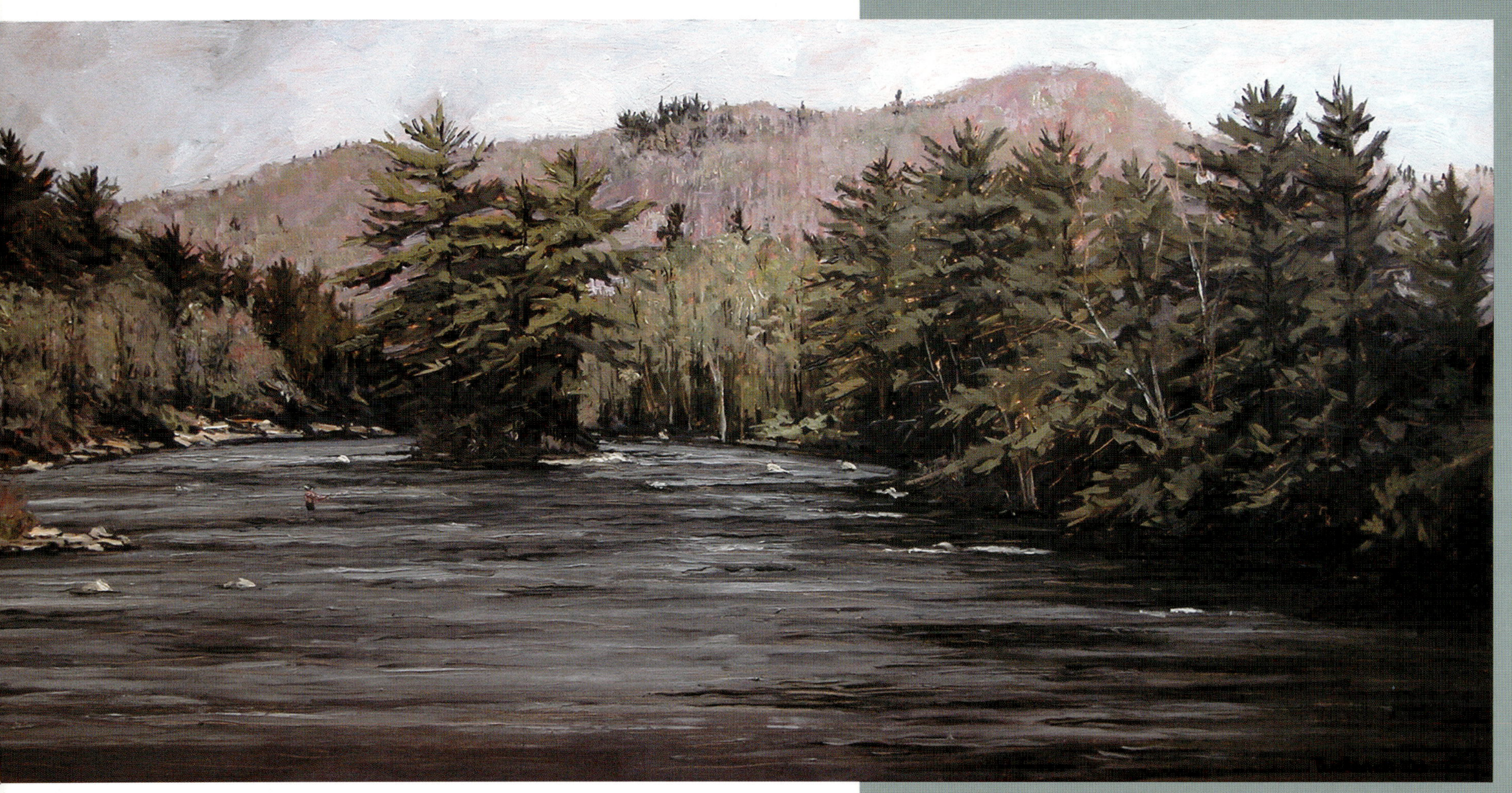

Emily Buchanan *Spring Along the Housatonic*

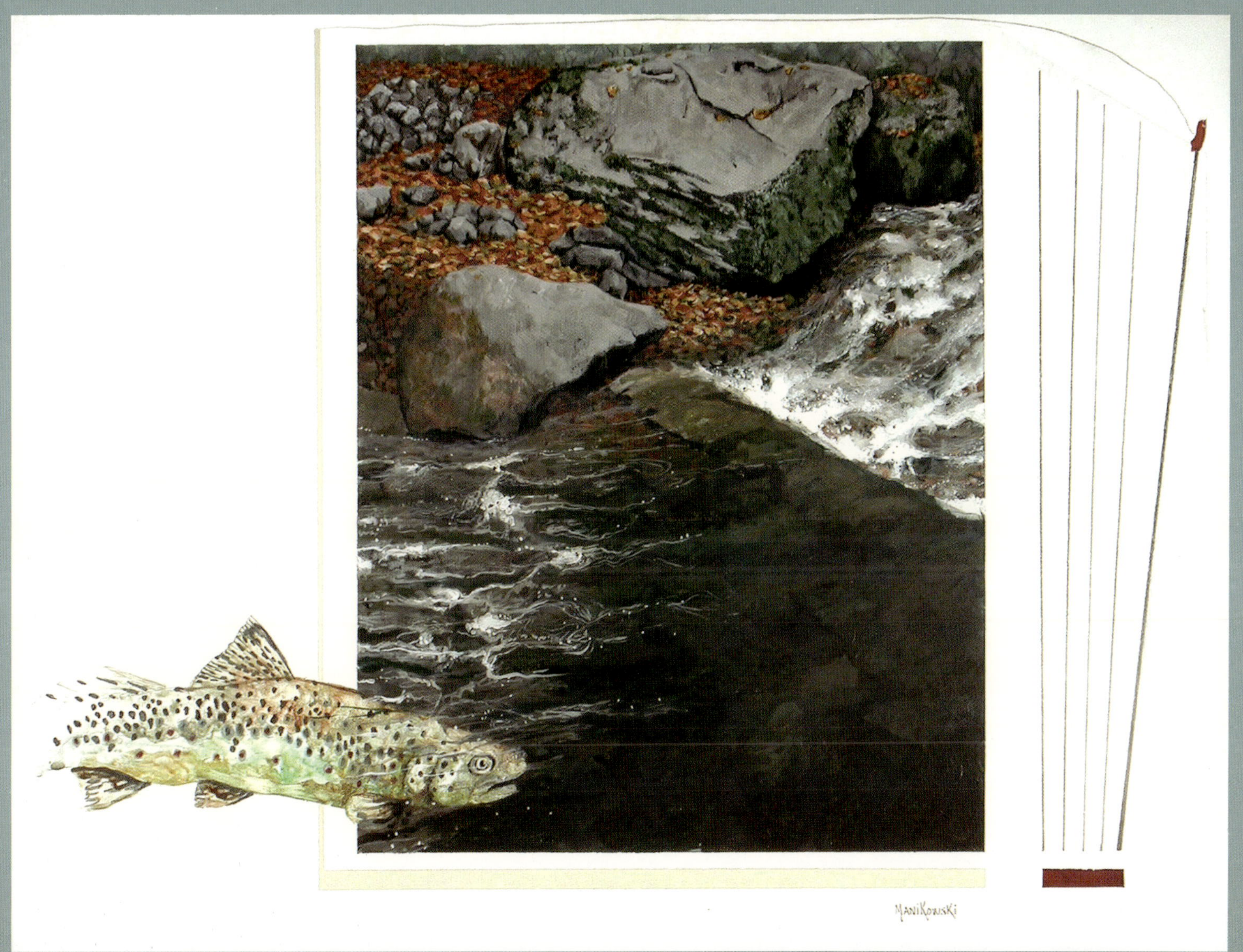

John **Manikowski** *River Pool with Trout*

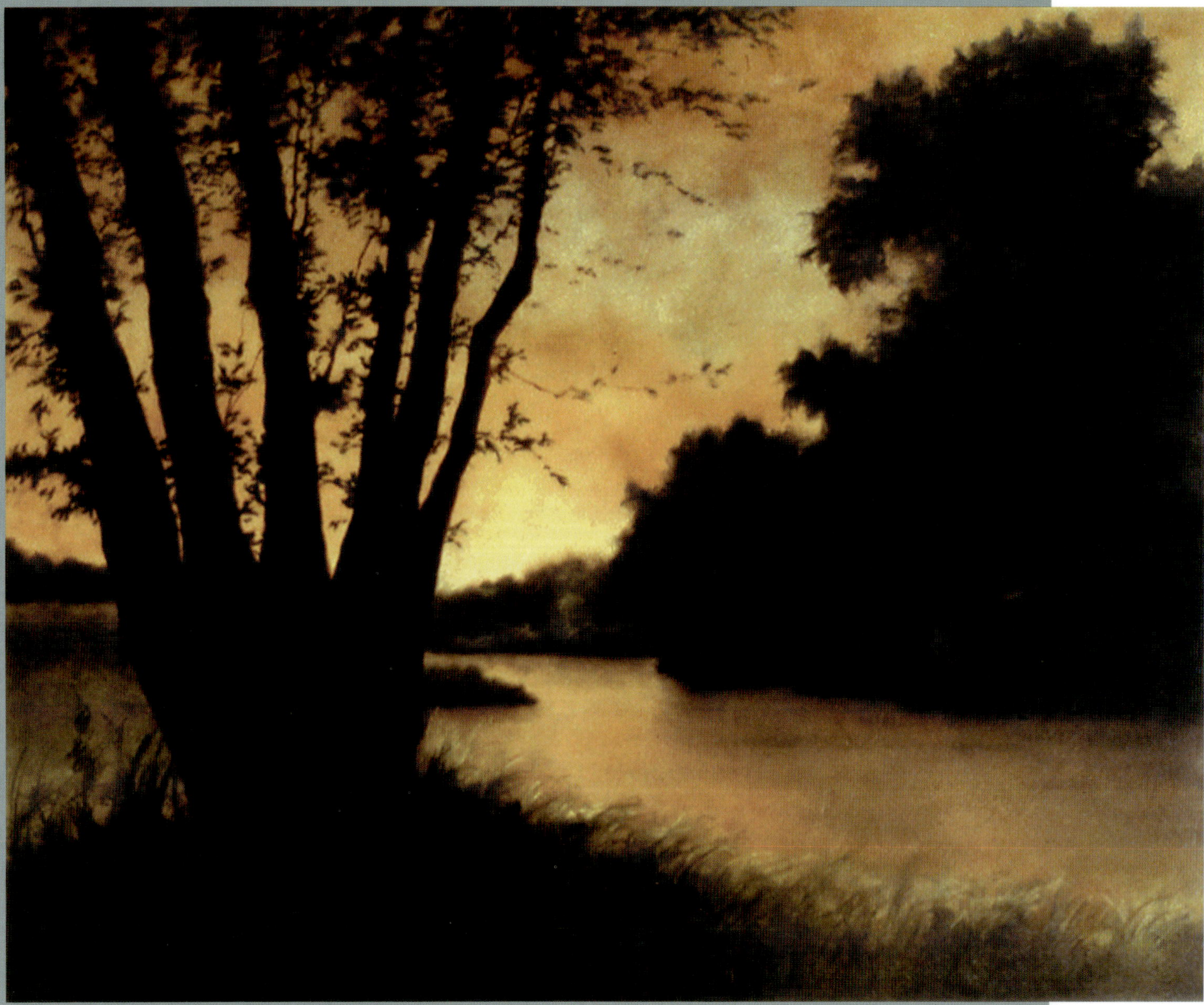

Gabrielle Senza   *Il Silenzio di Luce VII*

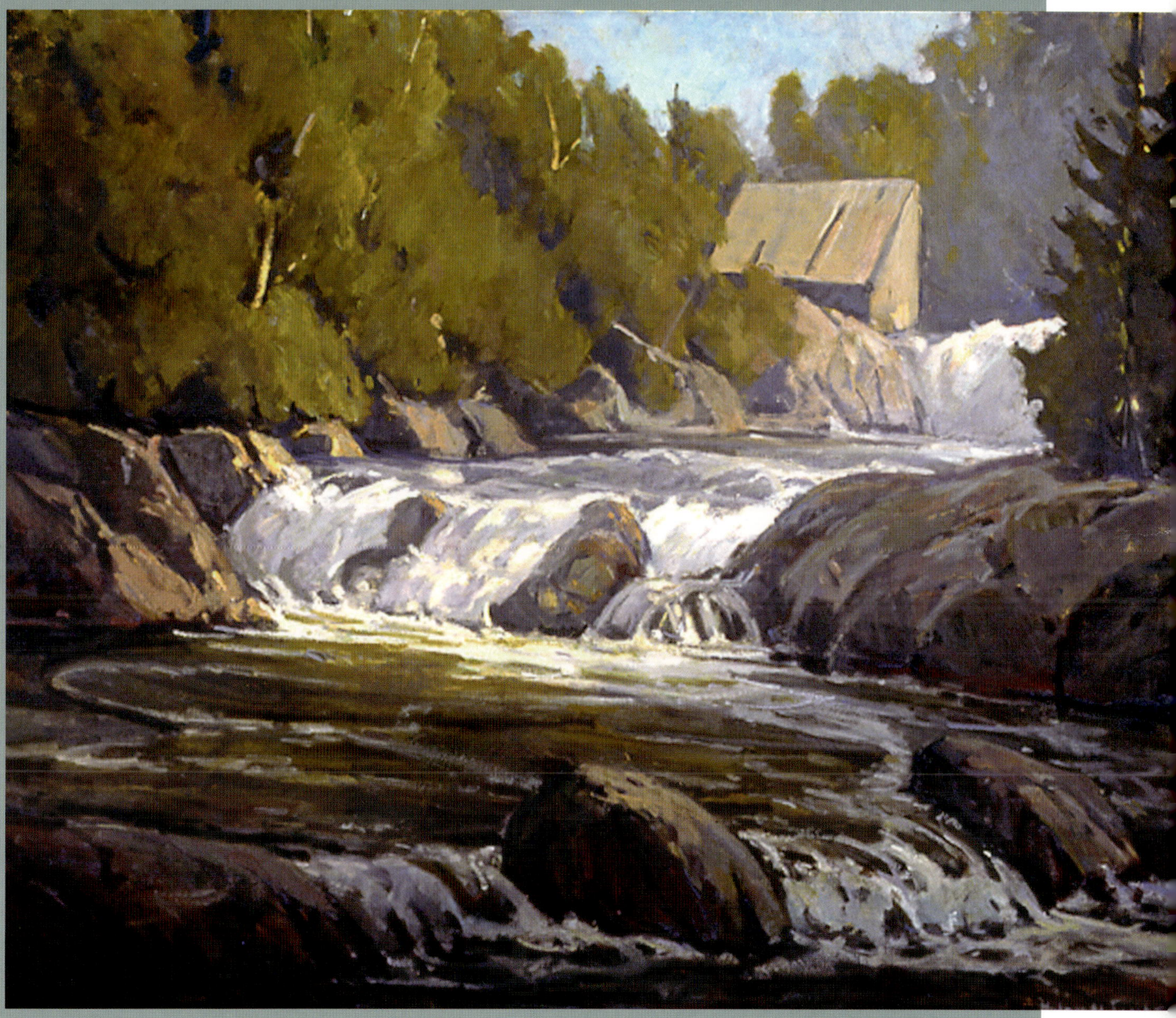

Helen Nichols Jacobs *Rushing Waters at Bull's Bridge*

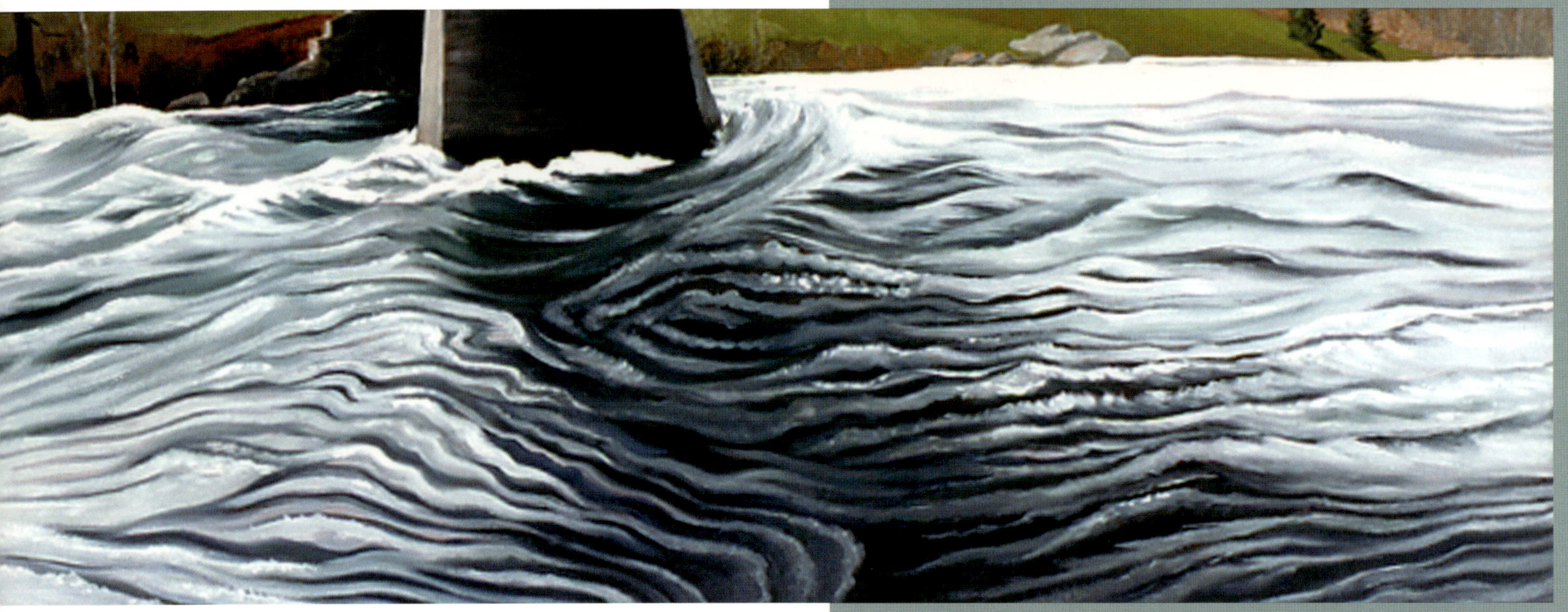

Erica Child Prud'homme *Under the Bridge: Spring Melt*

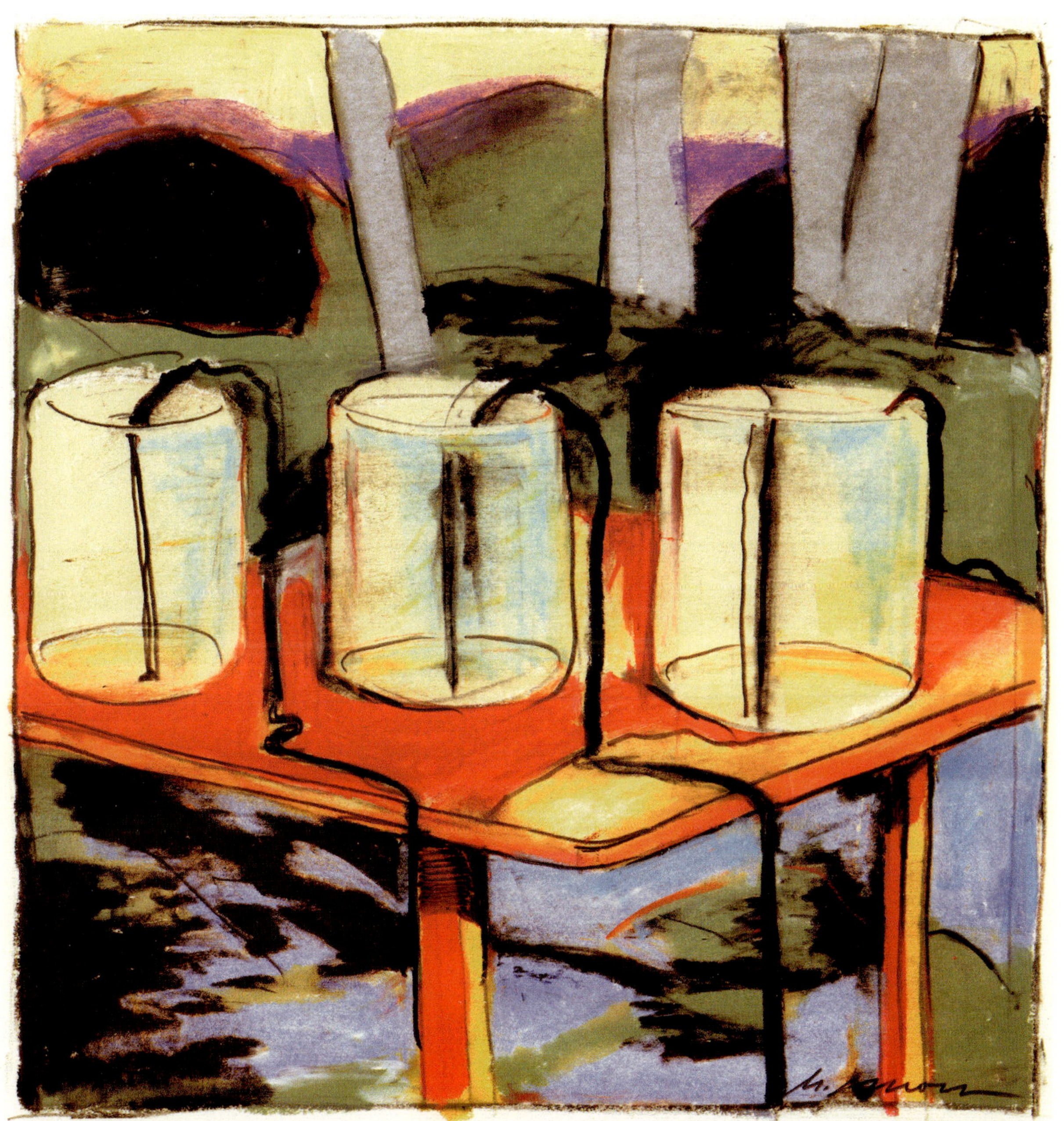

Geoffrey Moss *Three Beakers*

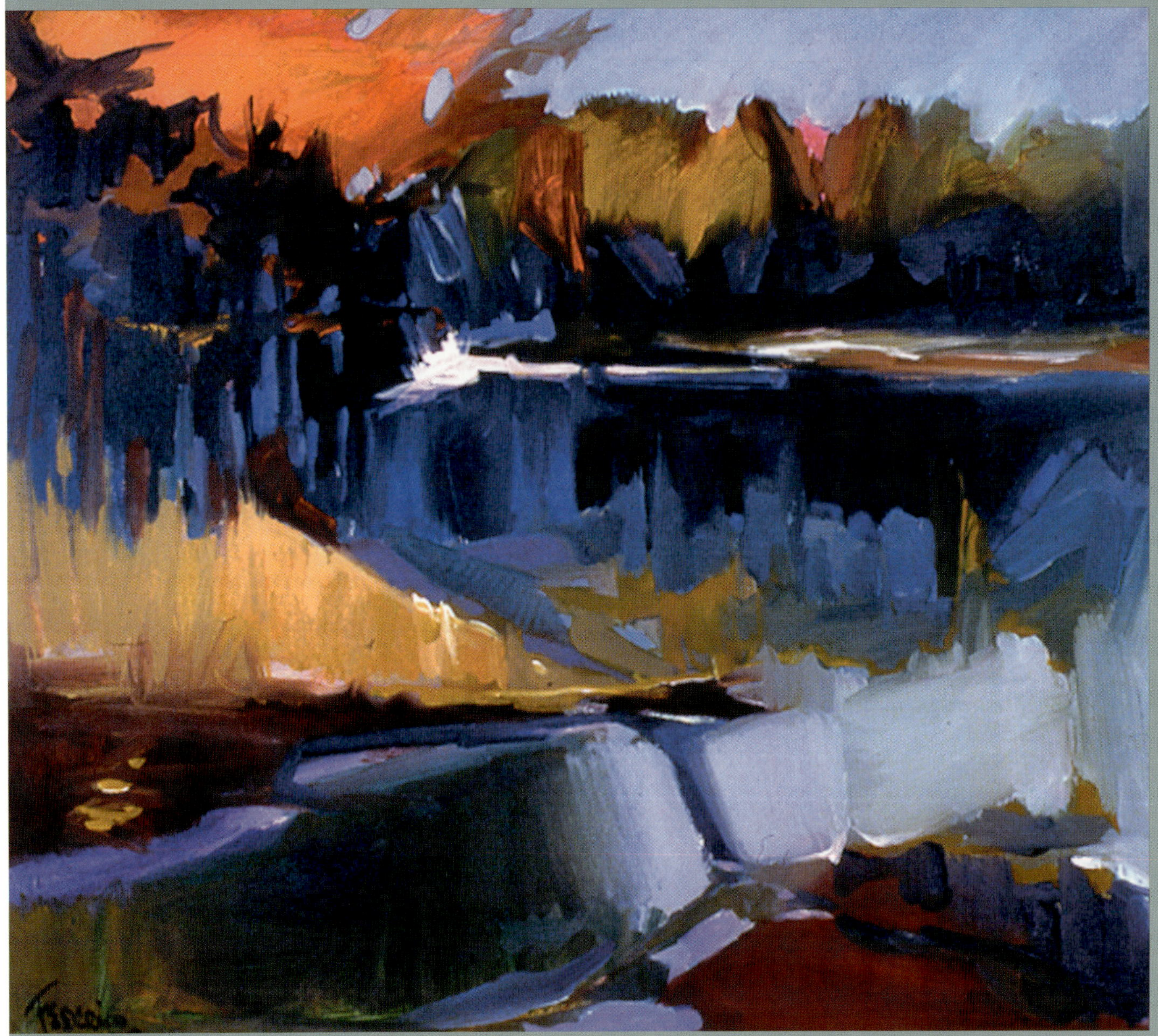

Frank Federico *River Bend*

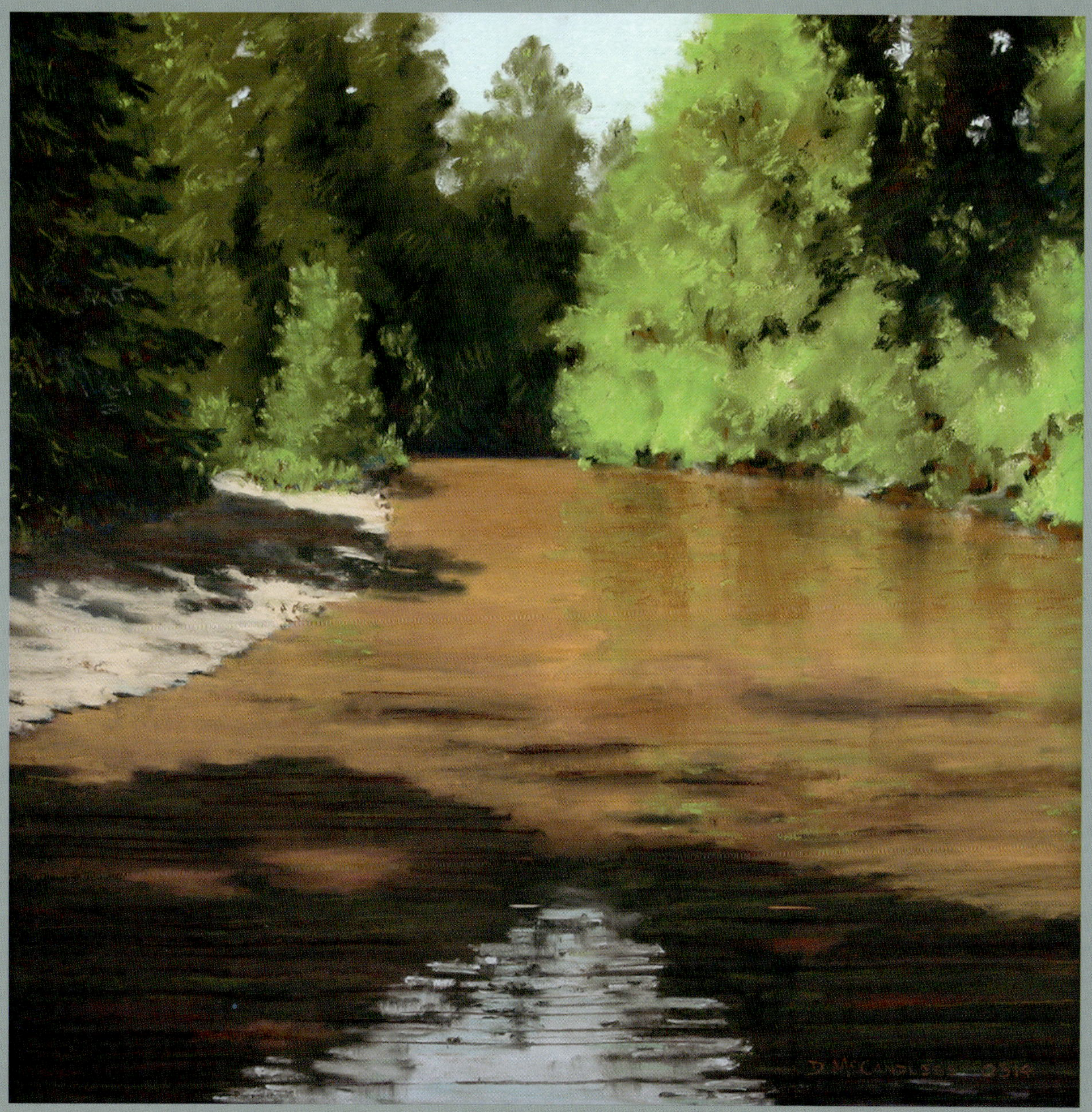

David McCandless *Housatonic Near Glendale*

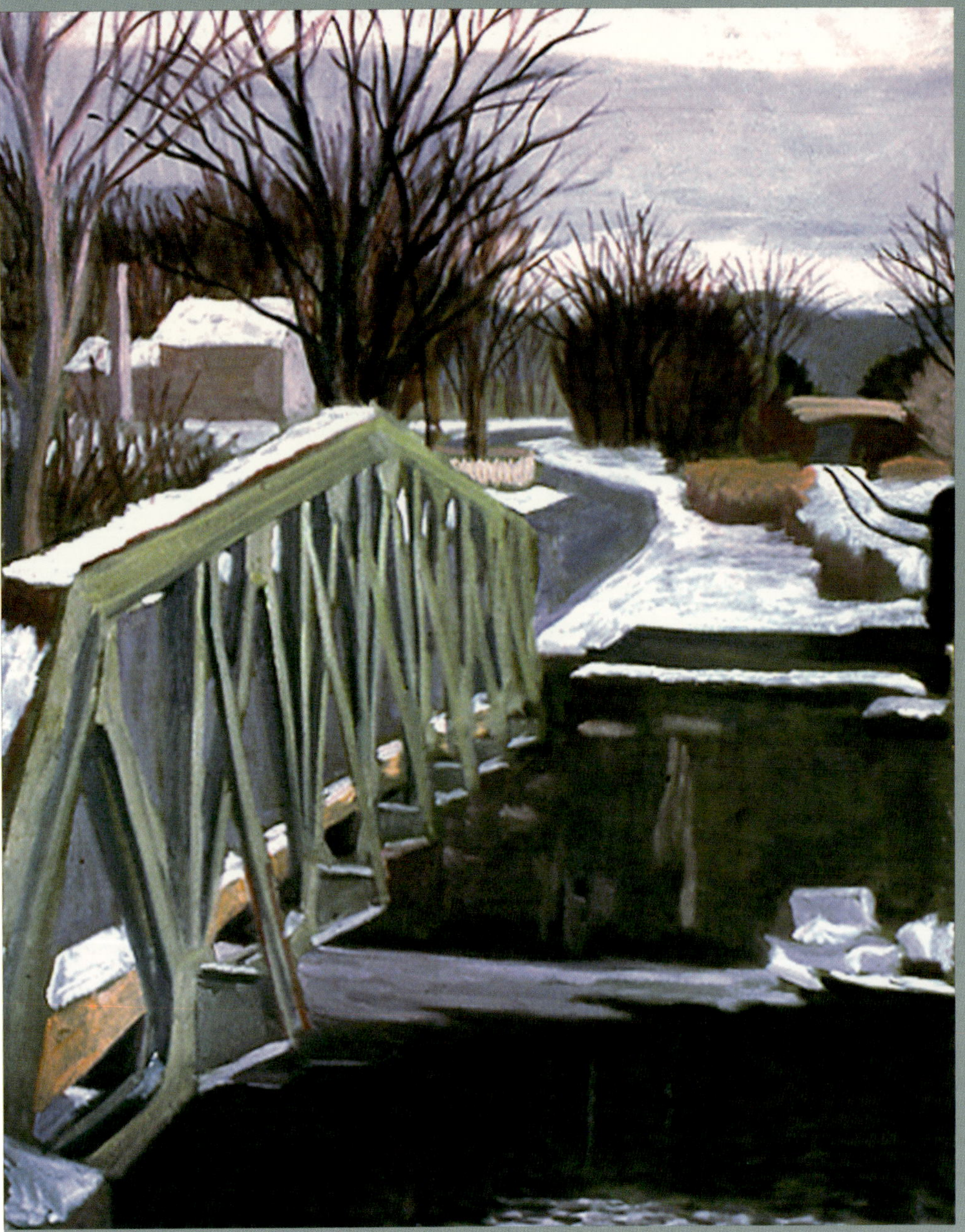

Margot Trout   *Green Bridge*

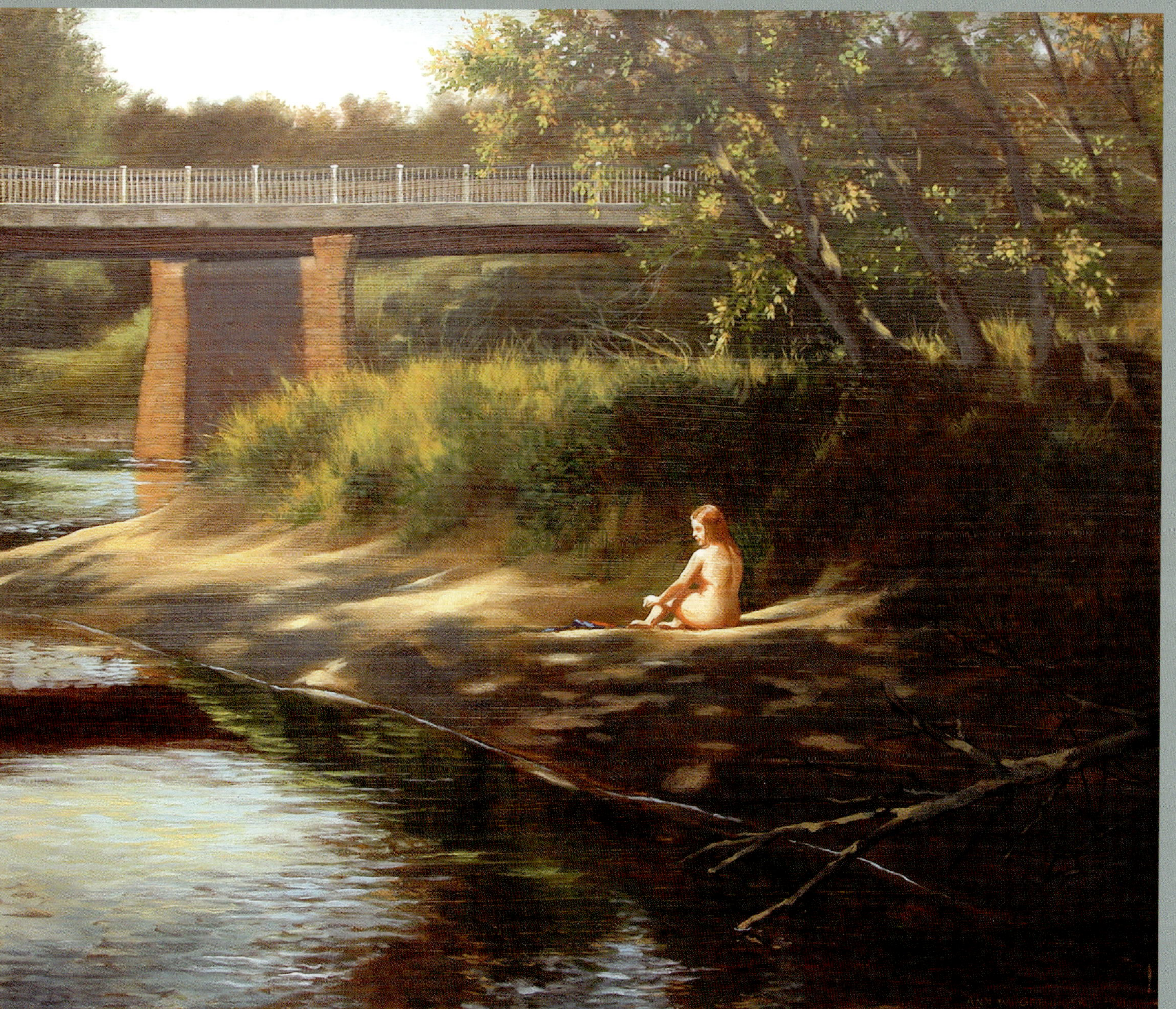

Ann Getsinger *Woman, River, and Bridge*

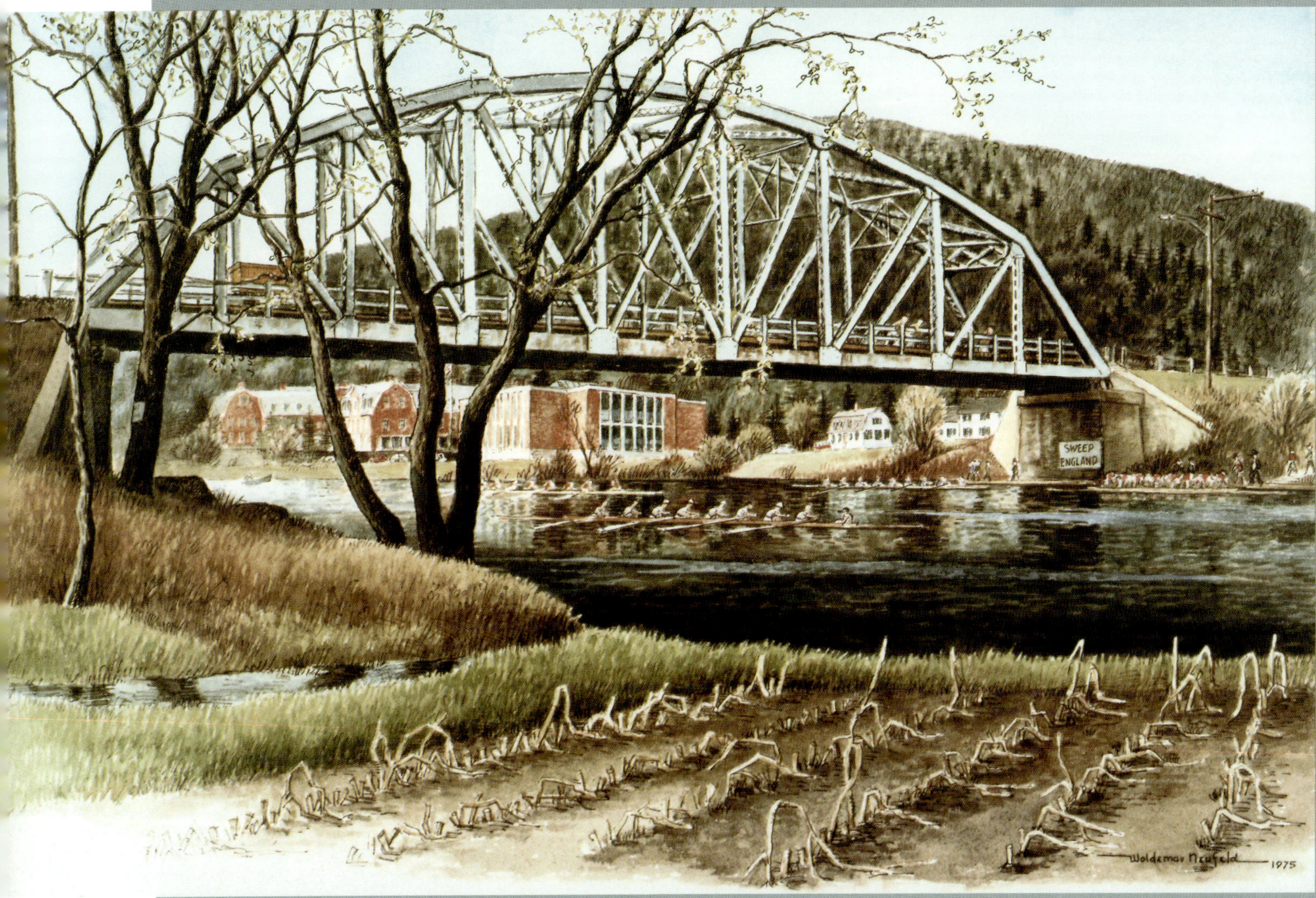

Woldemar Neufeld *Housatonic Bridge at Kent*

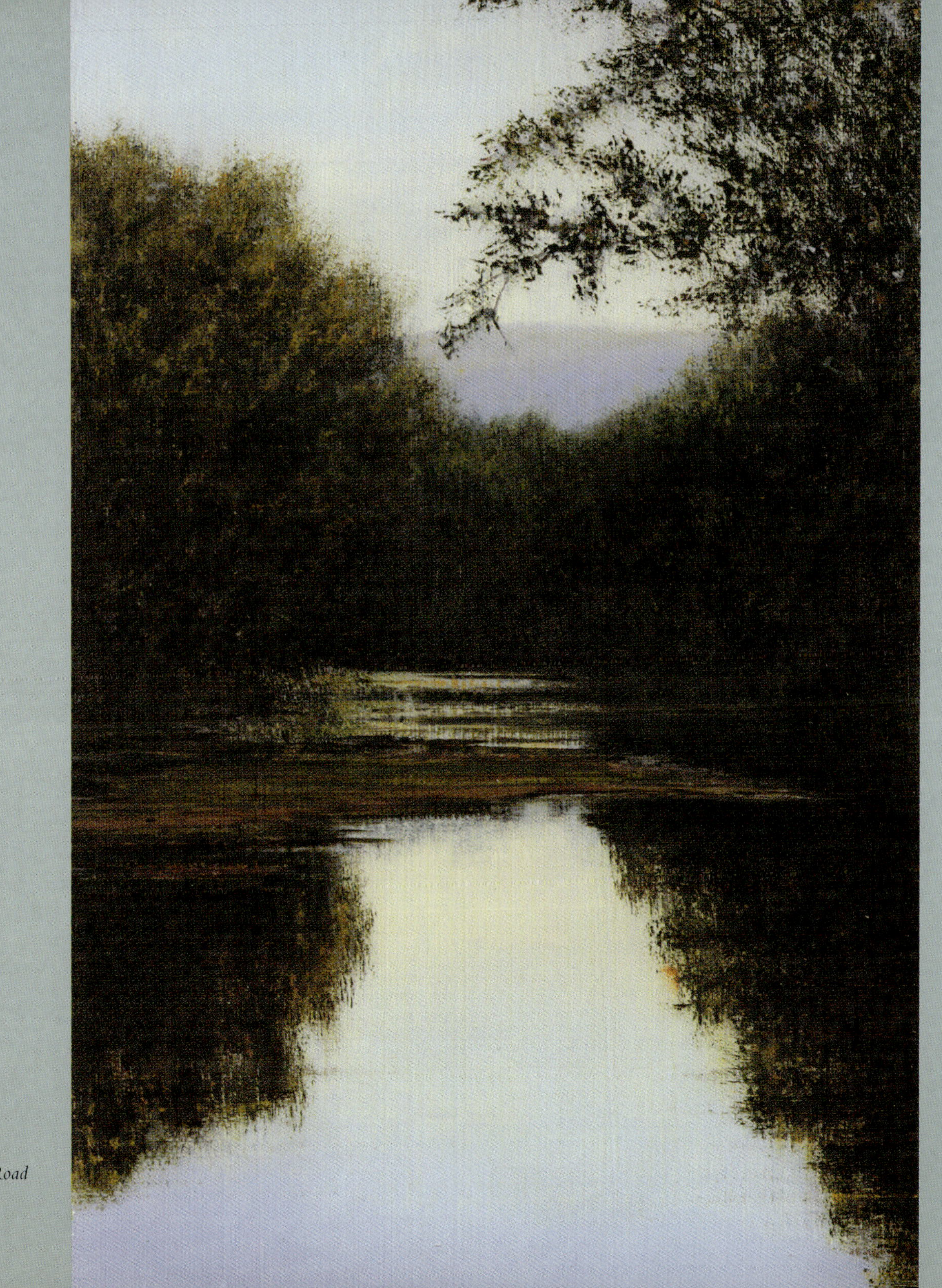

Bart Elsbach *Housatonic Bend from Kellogg Road*

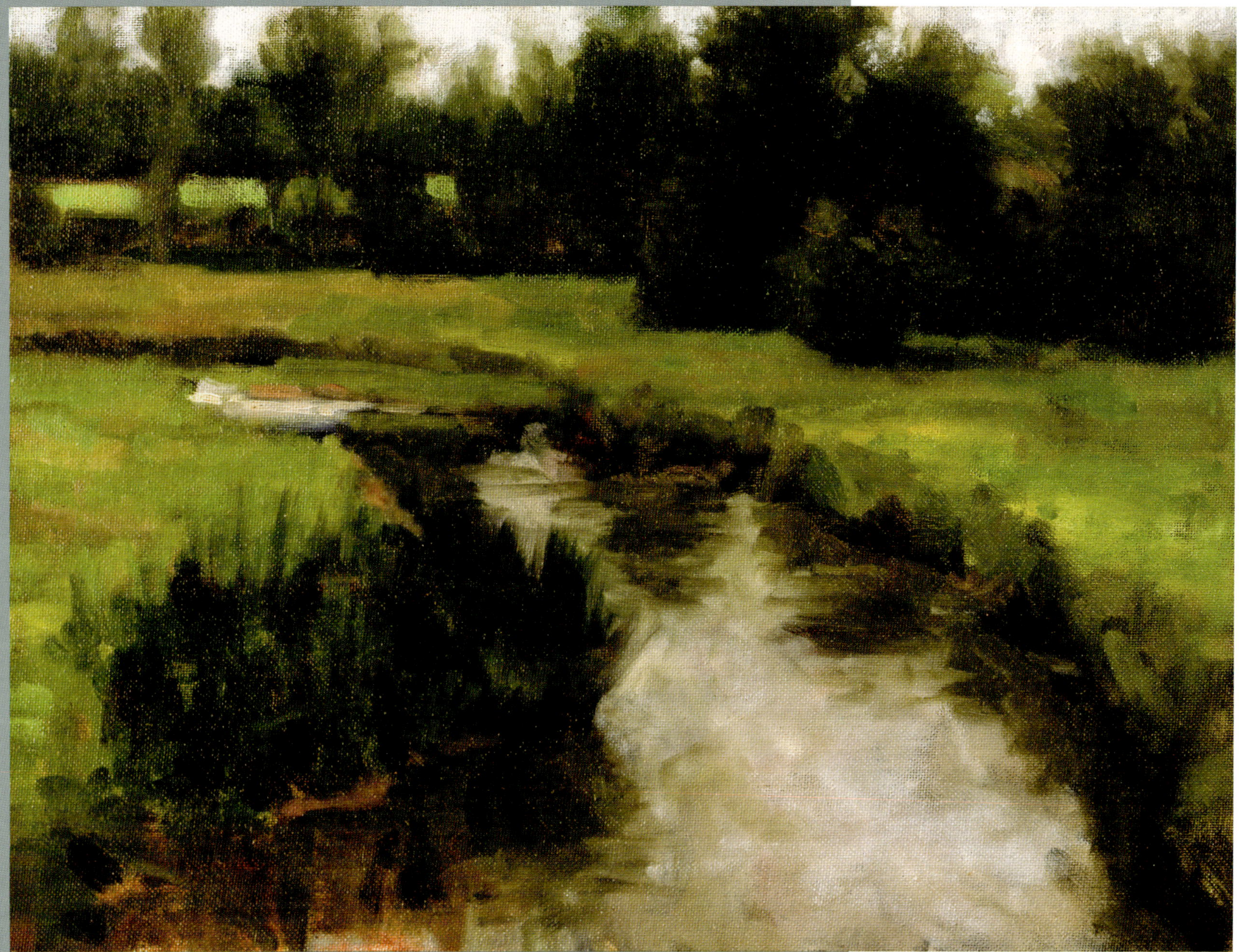

Joan Griswold *A Lazy River*

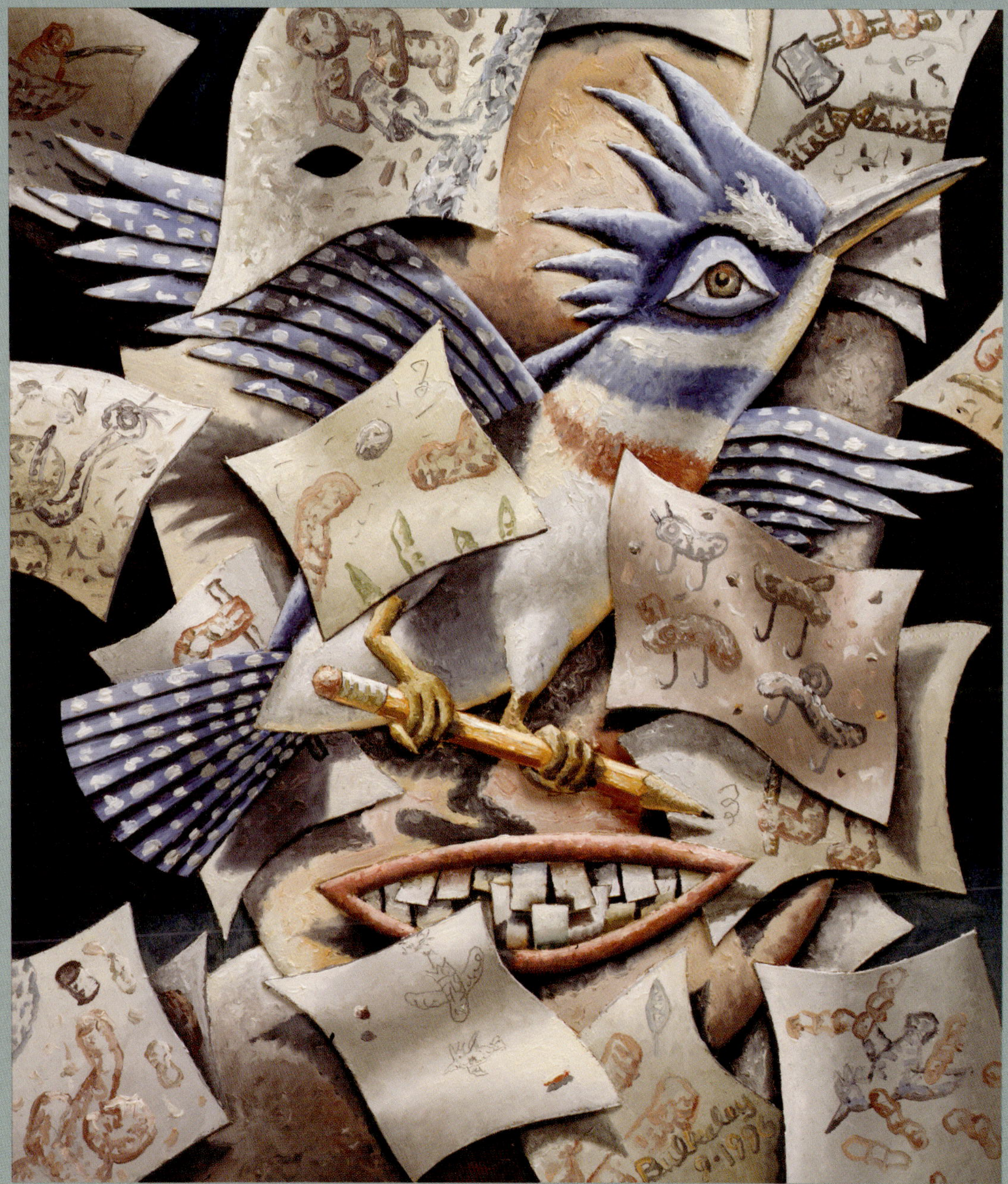

Morgan Bulkeley, Jr. *Kingfisher Sketches*

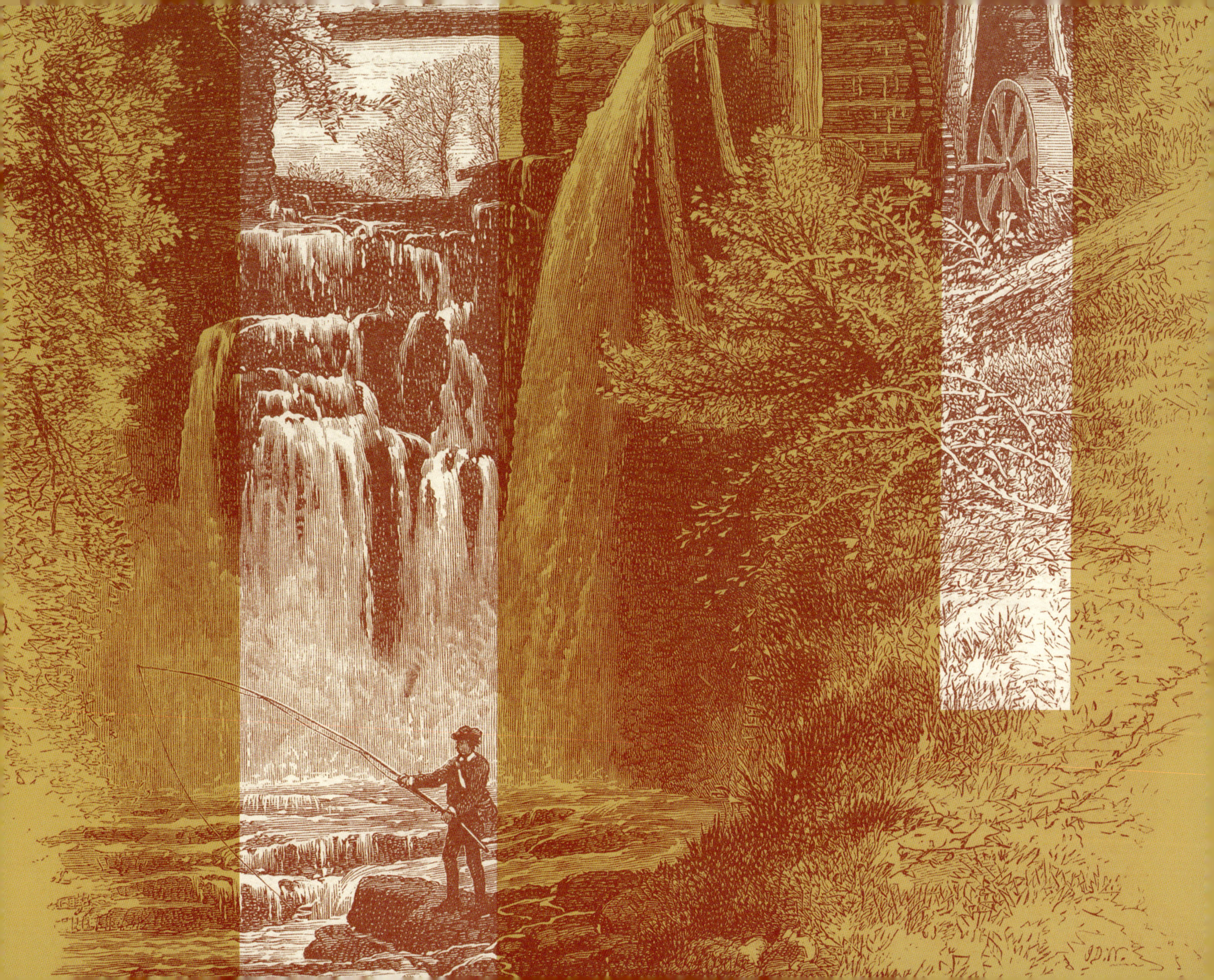

THE HOUSATONIC IS OUR RIVER

Eric Bruun

Long before the Housatonic River inspired an artist, or carried industrial chemicals downstream, the Housatonic was a place of wilderness. Soft peat, fallen limbs, soaring trees, calcareous swamps, fast-moving streams, and crystal-clear ponds framed the river. Dams did not impede its flow. Bridges did not cross or disrupt its current. Roads and houses and factories and farmers' fields did not infringe on the river's corridor.

Today, even the wildest-seeming features of the river, its tributaries, and its watershed have been shaped by the heavy hand of human intrusion. But as difficult as it is to imagine what this valley looked like 1,000 years ago, it is equally challenging to think of what the landscape was a century ago. Almost every tree on every hillside, valley, and plain had been felled to provide fuel for iron forges or to make way for farms. The river was a dank drain for a watershed that had been largely stripped of its natural resources.

We are lucky enough today to be around for the early stages of its renaissance as a natural feature. Ironically, the river's former smell and filth discouraged development for very long stretches. Nature was given the space to reclaim the water and riverbanks.

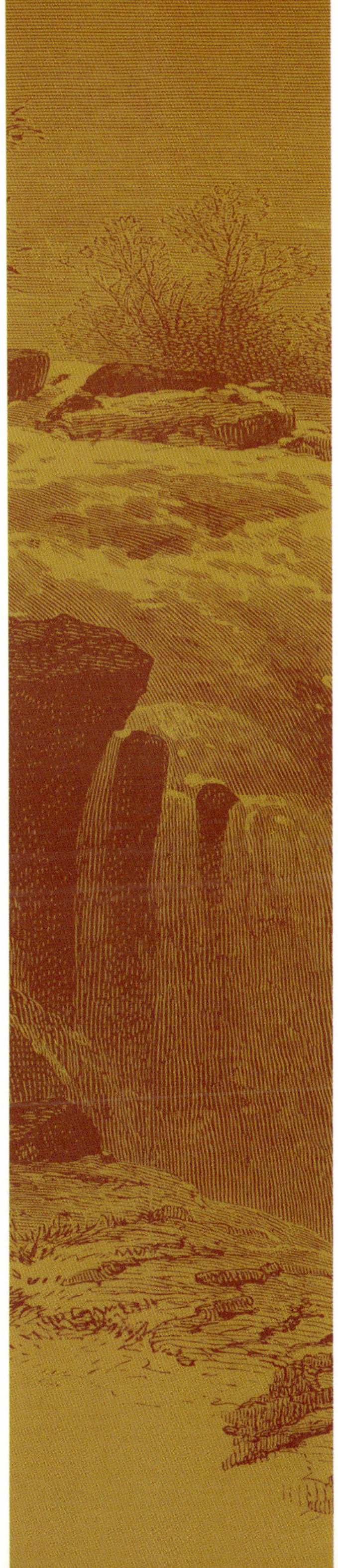

The Housatonic is now a beautiful river. But we must remember that underneath the pretty pictures of foliage, wildlife, and relatively clear water remain polychlorinated biphenyls (PCBs) that threaten to permanently stain the river.

More than 300 million years ago, a continental collision forged the hills and mountains of the eastern United States. The Housatonic River region was part of the Hudson River Valley. Geological shifts and glacial movements parted the two valleys about 50 million years ago.

The three streams that form the Housatonic converge near the center of Pittsfield, creating the main stem of the river. The Housatonic then heads almost due south for 132 miles with an overall drop of 959 feet. It empties into the Long Island Sound at Milford Point, Connecticut. The watershed covers nearly 2,000 square miles, including almost all of southern Berkshire County, most of northwestern Connecticut, and a small chunk of New York state.

Within the Upper Housatonic Valley are rare natural treasures. The Berkshire Taconic section along the state line between Massachusetts and Connecticut is one of the largest blocks of native natural habitats in the Northeast, its 36,000 acres the largest unfragmented forest in lower New England. Unusual deposits of limestone help create some of the most distinctive, diverse habitats in New England, including the floating mat of Kampoosa Bog in Stockbridge and wetlands rich in more than 100 rare plant and animal species along the Schenob Brook in Sheffield. Caves, marble ridges, lakes, and floodplain forests mark the Housatonic's flora and fauna in northwestern Connecticut.

Native Americans first arrived in the Housatonic Valley about 10,000 years ago. Archeologists believe they settled along the river, harvesting it for fish and farming its floodplains. When the first Dutch and British settlers arrived in the early 1700s they came upon the Mohican tribe of the Algonkian Indians.

The first European settlers used the river for utilitarian purposes. Its current powered mills and carried the waste of human activity downstream. Its water nurtured the frontier settlements from the outset.

Abundant high-quality iron ore in the Upper Housatonic Valley, especially in northwestern Connecticut, led to the rapid growth of iron forges. The iron industry began in Salisbury in 1734. By the 1800s, there were 40 blast furnaces from Lanesboro to Kent. The ore was smelted with limestone in the furnaces, which required huge amounts of charcoal to keep aflame. Iron tools, utensils, and weapons were forged from the ore and cooled in the Housatonic.

The Housatonic Railroad was one of the first railroads of any length in the United States. Built in the early 1840s along the river, it carried local iron products to serve the national economy. Northwestern Connecticut was envisioned as the Pittsburgh of the United States before there was a Pittsburgh.

Extensive marble and limestone deposits were quarried. The Washington Monument, New York's City Hall, and the Boston Custom House all include marble from Sheffield. Also in the 1800s, paper mills flourished, especially in the Pittsfield area. Zenas Crane established the first paper mill in Dalton in 1801. Powered by the Housatonic River, the mills became the first paper producers to serve a national market. Crane Paper today produces the paper used in U.S. currency.

Despite the growth of industry, the nineteenth-century image of the Berkshires remained "the place by itself" that so attracted artists and writers. Political and cultural leaders were starting to articulate an American identity in which nature was a manifestation of divine will: every natural fact was a symbol of some spiritual fact. The landscape was celebrated in writing, music,

and painting. The area's mountains, streams, fields, and winding river were praised as the idyllic region where one could find balance with nature. William Cullen Bryant, who served as Great Barrington's town clerk before becoming a nationally known newspaper editor in New York City, described it as a region not surpassed in picturesque loveliness. In poems such as "Monument Mountain" he described the region in divine terms:

> Thou who woulds't see the lovely and the wild,
> Mingled in harmony on Nature's face,
> Ascend our rocky mountains.

Herman Melville responded from his Pittsfield home to Nathaniel Hawthorne in a July 22, 1851, letter: "I thank you for your easy-flowing long letter… which flowed through me, and refreshed all my meadows, as the Housatonic—opposite me—does in reality."

The nationally acclaimed actress Fanny Kemble wrote in 1835 from Lenox: "The Valley of the Housatonic, locked in by walls of every shape and size from grassy knolls to bold basaltic cliffs—a 'Happy Valley' indeed! A beautiful little river wanders singing from side to side in this secluded paradise."

As Lenox and Stockbridge emerged as summer destinations for some of the wealthiest families in the United States during the late nineteenth century, so did the Housatonic River Valley's prominence as a place of leisure and relaxation.

But the experience of the river itself diverged from the reputation of its valley. Small factories used water up and down the river for power and as a dumping ground for waste products. The river carried away sewage from pipes sticking out from behind homes.

In 1894, William Stanley demonstrated the first successful alternating current transformer from his small factory on the banks of the Housatonic in Great Barrington, one reason it was the first town in America to be electrified. He opened a factory in Pittsfield four years later that was eventually bought by General Electric. The Pittsfield plant became a major electrical equipment factory, employing as many as 14,000 people. At some point, GE started to dispose of PCBs in the conveniently located river.

The effluent from the GE plant, dozens of paper and pulp companies, textile factories, and other industries took a profound toll on the river. By the 1960s, children were warned by their parents not to go near the Housatonic River because of the filth and pollution it carried. Residents in Lee tell stories about how they could see what was happening at the paper mills upstream by the color of the river.

As the environmental movement emerged, the course of the Housatonic River started to turn. Federal clean water laws in the 1970s ended the dumping of pollutants into the river. Grassroots organizations began to organize river cleanups. The Berkshire Natural Resources Council organized the Upper Housatonic Wildlife Management Area along the river in Massachusetts, and the Housatonic Valley Association secured large corridors of protected land in Connecticut.

The reputation of the Housatonic River began to change as it started to become a cleaner waterway. Berkshire residents began to recognize the Housatonic as an asset to the community and not a liability.

One last toxic, almost invisible, stain remains in the river, however. The Housatonic River in Pittsfield and Lenox is one of the largest PCB contamination sites in the nation. Starting in 1992, the Housatonic River Initiative has battled GE and encouraged local

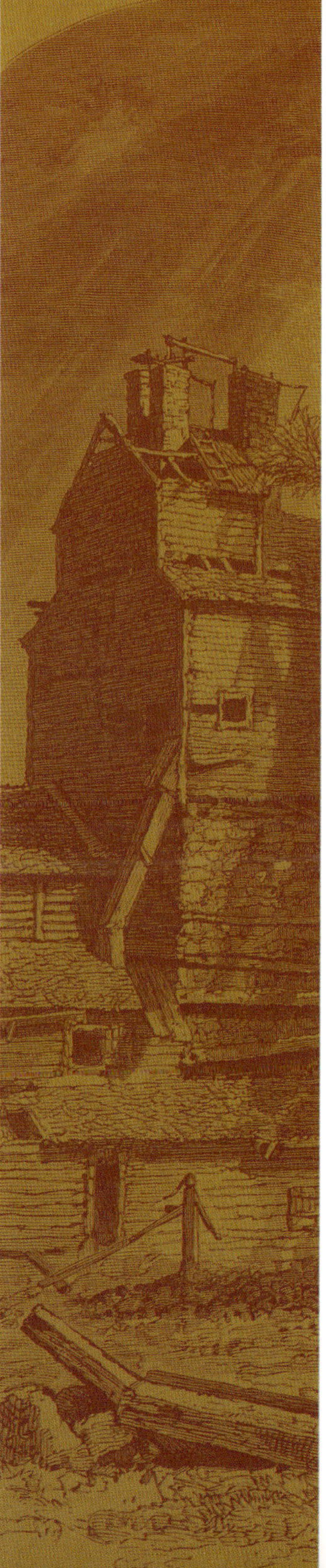

communities to pressure the company to do a complete cleanup of the toxic waste, which is believed to cause cancer. In a controversial settlement with the U.S. Environmental Protection Agency, GE was forced to implement major remediation efforts in the first six miles downstream from its Pittsfield facility.

Housatonic River Initiative is now bracing for a final effort to compel the EPA to impose a similar cleanup farther south to Rising Pond in Great Barrington.

PCBs are heavy molecules that tend to sink into the mud behind dams and in slow-moving parts of the river. Though contaminated sediments downstream from Lenox are relatively low compared with the Pittsfield section, those PCB levels still exceed the federal standards that would allow people to have safe contact with the Housatonic, much less eat fish from it. Even in Connecticut, the fish that bring fly fishers from around the world to the Houstatonic cannot be eaten.

Nevertheless, the Housatonic is once again an appealing river. Many people sing its glories as a source of inspiration and beauty.

But it is really quite a small river—almost inconsequential in the greater scheme. In its smallness, however, we find an intimacy with nature that cannot be found in the great rivers of the nation. At the end of the day, the Housatonic River is an important river because it is our river.

Erik Bruun lives in Great Barrington with his wife and two children. He helped to found the Housatonic River Initiative and has written a "people restoration plan" for Housatonic River Restoration.

CLEANING UP

George S. Wislocki

I first set foot on the banks of the Housatonic River in the mid–1960s. We had moved from a home that overlooked the Hudson River to a house on Church Street in Stockbridge that fronted on the Housatonic. My new neighbor, an elderly and practical man, dumped his yard waste and the unburnable portion of his household trash into the river. I informed him that this was not an acceptable environmental practice and was probably illegal. He looked at me for some time with genuine bewilderment before replying that this was a trash river, as though it had been so classified by a special legislative designation.

Weeks later, I took my first canoe trip on the river, and I had to conclude that he might well have been speaking for many of our neighbors. Whole reaches of the river were nothing more than heaps of trash stranded on fallen trees and other snags. In the early morning mist, these obstacles could look like the shrouded channel markers on the crossings of the River Styx. The river in those days could be a fearful place.

By that time, a small group of river loyalists, which had incorporated as the Housatonic River Watershed Association, was meeting regularly at the home of Francis (Cissy) Paddock in Lenox. The group was formed by Joyce Crane of Dalton. Both women played a prominent role in local garden clubs. These clubs,

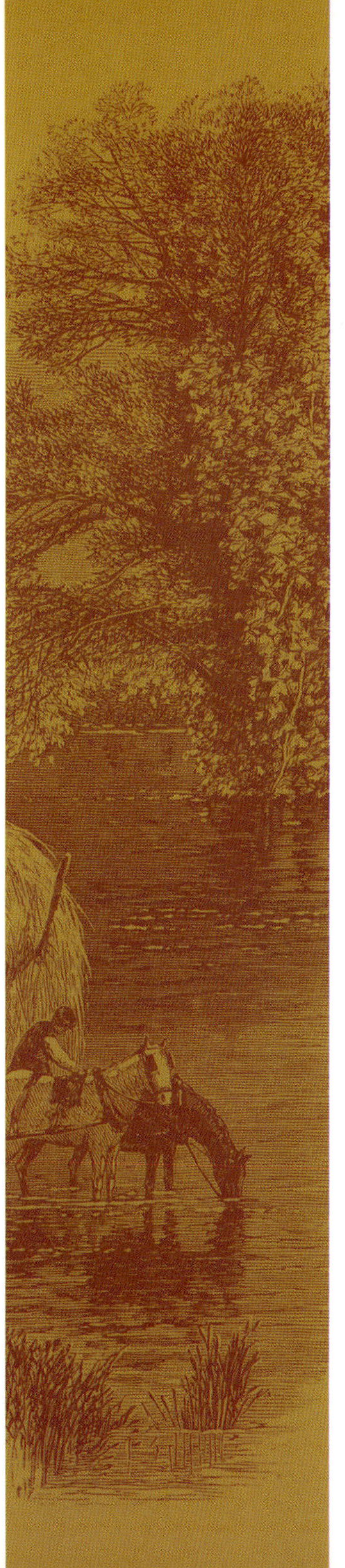

along with the League of Women Voters, were the original Berkshire stewards for conservation and for river protection in particular.

Regulars at the meetings included Joan Flood, president of the League; Betty Phinney, a Massachusetts Audubon Society schoolteacher who loved to bring baskets filled with nature into classrooms; Charlie Liston, a land surveyor who lived in Lenoxdale and seemed to think of the river as an old friend who always needed help; and George (Gig) Darey, who was Lenox's Tree Warden, chairman of the Lenox Conservation Commission, and soon to become chairman of the Commonwealth's Board of Fisheries and Wildlife. Gig, a passionate hunter, always reminded me that there was a time when you could see more duck blinds on the river than houses. He went on to win many awards, but none from the Massachusetts Homebuilders Association.

The meetings were also attended by two local naturalists—Alvah Sanborn, director of the Pleasant Valley Sanctuary, and Morgan Bulkeley, a writer who in those days lived in Mount Washington and wrote about the river in a column that appeared weekly in The Berkshire Eagle under the title "Our Berkshires." I was probably the youngest member of this group.

The meetings were usually devoted to organizing river cleanup days on which volunteers would pull out shopping carts, tires, and the other debris that had been dumped into the river. This task is never finished, since trash always seems to find its way back into the river. But still and all, there is a lot less of it in the river than there used to be. Massachusetts did a lot for the river the day it required a deposit on bottles and cans.

Cleanup days, particularly those involving schoolchildren, were very important in building a constituency for the river. They continue today in one form or another, and any list of the river rats involved will be incomplete. One of my favorites was Lon

Nordeen, a wonderfully inventive man from Pittsfield who liked to place large sweep booms across the river to catch debris before it ended up on snags, the only hitch being that the booms often broke loose and ended up downriver on one or another snag themselves. Lon has crossed the river long ago, but he left behind a lasting memorial by deeding to the Commonwealth a wonderful wetlands at the headwaters of Richmond Pond. So it is that he truly does belong to the river.

Then there is Court McDermott, also from Pittsfield, the founder and principal organizer of the annual Great Upper Housatonic Canoe Race. The event, held throughout the 80s, required that, in preparation for the race, every fallen tree must be removed from the river for a distance of six miles. They may have been the only six miles of unobstructed water for the river's entire distance.

Michael Makes, another Pittsfield resident, to this day organizes river cleanup days when the mood suits him. His schedule for these happenings is governed by some celestial calendar known only to him.

Cleanup days removed tons and tons of trash from the Housatonic. But the most lasting achievement of the Housatonic River Watershed Association was to plan and build support for the Upper Housatonic Wildlife Management Area, a greenbelt that protects the banks of the river from the center of Pittsfield into northern Lee. This wonderful green corridor was first suggested at these meetings and was realized through the efforts of the Massachusetts Audubon Society (with their Canoe Meadows Sanctuary), the Massachusetts Division of Fisheries and Wildlife (which owns most of the public land in this area), and the Lenox Conservation Commission. The Berkshire Natural Resources Council often proved helpful to these groups by negotiating gifts of land that were then consolidated and turned over to

the Commonwealth and others. Today, I believe that this natural area is not only important to wildlife, it is tangible proof that a few hard-working people can make great improvements in their own community.

The 1960s and '70s were all about building a constituency for the river. During that time, the most influential agent for river change was Morgan Bulkeley. His columns in the Eagle were religiously read by those who would gather by the river on cleanup days, as well as by community leaders. Morgan was a strong and persistent voice for the river. I think he saw it as a small, wonderful natural system that always glittered in the morning light, but at the same time he reminded us that it is also part of a landscape that has suffered generations of abuse.

Getting rid of the trash in the trash river was only part of the job. The Housatonic was also highly contaminated with sewage and industrial waste. Rivers have a great capacity to buffer and cure themselves from human waste. However, when an entire community's raw sewage is introduced to a river in a season of low flow, the river's ecosystem is likely to collapse. And against some industrial waste, natural systems are defenseless.

After passage in 1972 of the federal legislation and subsequent amendments that became known as the Clean Water Act, communities began building sewage treatment plants that adequately protected the Housatonic. The act also required that industries stop dumping thousands of gallons of contaminated waste.

In the mid-'70s we learned that the industrial damage inflicted on the Housatonic over the years might be irreparable. The PCBs that General Electric fed into the river for more than 40 years at Pittsfield now contaminated the entire river, all the way down to Long Island Sound.

Our generation of river loyalists and neighborhood

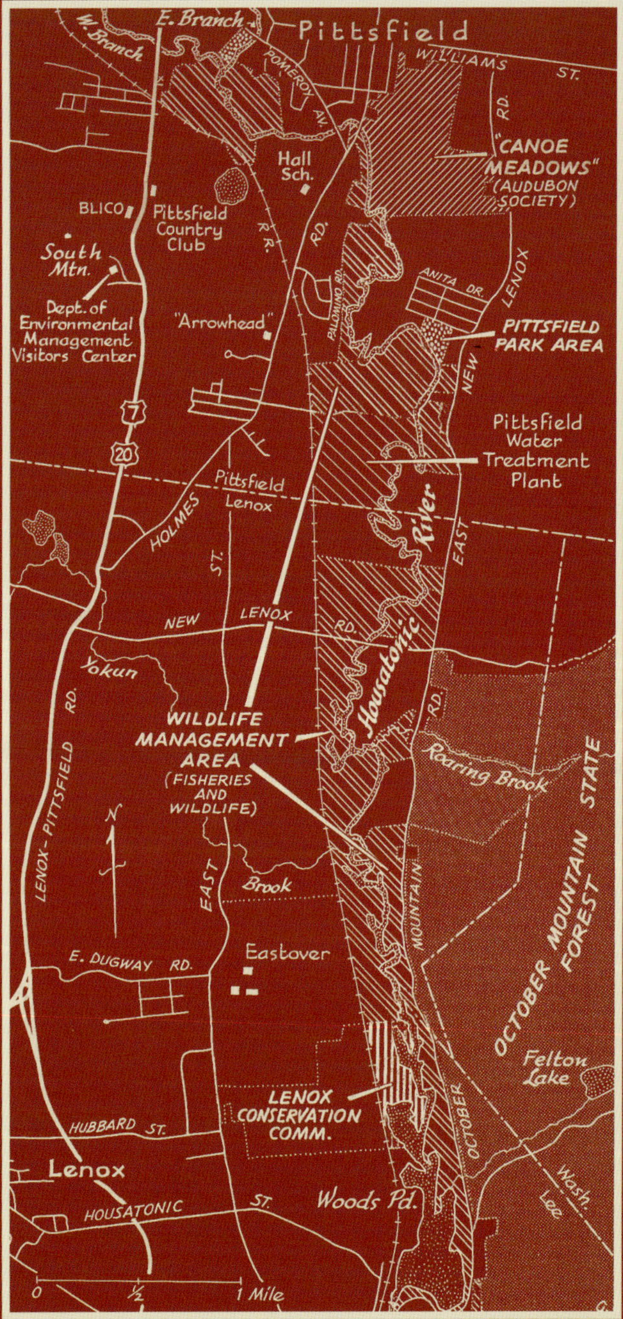

advocates already knew that GE was no friend to the Housatonic River. Cross any bridge in Pittsfield and you would likely see an oily sheen from seepage beneath the GE plant. Pittsfield was a one-company town, and most residents remained indifferent to GE's crimes against nature. After the PCB contamination became known, the most outspoken resident was Remo (Ray) DelGallo, former mayor of Pittsfield and owner of a tavern located between the GE plant and the east branch of the river. Ray demanded that GE take responsibility for cleaning up many of his neighbors' properties, which were awash in PCB-laden oils. He and Massachusetts State Representative Chris Hodgkin were the only local politicians to take the lead in challenging GE.

What finally brought public outcry was not the scientific evidence showing that PCBs were carcinogens, but the fact that GE had deliberately misled everyone—employees, neighbors, and regulators—as to the extent of contamination. Then, residents of contaminated Pittsfield neighborhoods and former GE employees, such as Ed Bates, joined in calling for a cleanup of the city neighborhoods and the river.

If a single moment serves as a bookmark for the story of the river's cleanup, it would be a photograph that appeared in The Berkshire Eagle in 1992 of Benno Friedman, a river activist, passing in his kayak in front of a huge embankment of trash from Pittsfield's landfill that was eroding into the river. Later it was discovered that this landfill was a major burial ground for drums containing a broad array of toxic waste. The drums originated at GE and had been delivered to their burial ground in off-hours.

Map of the Upper Housatonic Wildlife Management Area, a greenbelt organized by the Houstatonic River Watershed Association that runs from Pittsfield to Lee

Months later, a gathering was held at the West Stockbridge Sportmen's Club that eventually led to the organization of the Housatonic River Initiative, which has effectively served as Berkshires' environmental voice on this issue since the early '90s.

Luckily for the river, a new generation of environmental regulators came to the fore in Boston during the 1990s. Doug Luckerman, Al Weinberg, Lynn Cutler, Bryan Olson and others at the U.S. Environmental Protection Agency developed the regulatory strategy that was used to challenge GE and, ultimately, bring about the cleanup of the neighborhoods and the river. John DeVillars, President Clinton's newly appointed EPA regional administrator, decided that cleaning up the Housatonic would be his first priority for all of New England. John is a man who loves a fight, and GE—with its legion of lawyers and its arrogant CEO, Jack Welch—represented the perfect challenge. His most important accomplishment may have been to provide an opportunity for local government, neighborhoods, and the press to have substantial access to the decision-making process. By doing so, he built the case for river cleanup not only in the media but with the politicians and, most importantly, with the people of Pittsfield.

Today, most of the PCBs have been removed from the river adjacent to the old plant but the chemical still contaminates much of the river downstream. There are many drawbacks to removing soil contaminated with PCBs, not the least of which is what to do with it once it has been removed. It is probably safe to say that GE will vigorously oppose any substantive cleanup of the river. GE, however, is now faced with scientific evidence that PCBs are slowly destroying the river's aquatic food chain and that this devastation is reaching

into populations of mink, otters, and other animals that live on food from the river.

The river has a large and active constituency whose members think and work daily on its behalf. Dennis Regan heads the Housatonic Valley Association's Berkshire programs and has built a splendid coalition of Massachusetts "stream teams" that are steadfast in their dedication to monitoring the river's condition. Housatonic River Initiative, led by Tim Gray of Lee, was made River Keeper by Riverwatch, the conservation organization led by Robert Kennedy, Jr. Rachel Fletcher directs the Housatonic River Restoration, a consortium of many towns and environmental groups. Rachel is also the creator of River Walk, which has built a lovely and exuberant path that lets you walk along the bank of the river behind all those buildings that barricade Main Street of Great Barrington from its river. If Tim is the river keeper, surely Rachel is the caretaker, at least for the Massachusetts portion of the river.

I would like to believe that the Housatonic, once dismissed as a trash river, is viewed today as a wonderful asset, a blessing for all who are lucky enough to live in Berkshire or Litchfield counties. Among other evidence that this may be the case, there is a proposal to build a public walkway along the river just below the GE plant and only a few hundred feet from my home, which prompts me to believe that there are many today who would agree with Morgan Bulkeley that our small river does indeed glitter in the morning light.

George S. Wislocki was founder and first president of the Berkshire Natural Resources Council. For more than 30 years, he saw to the acquisition and protection of many acres throughout the Berkshires. He remains a staunch advocate for the Housatonic River.

MORGAN BULKELEY, A VOICE FOR THE RIVER

Jon Swan

While artists working in other media sought to capture the beauty of the Housatonic, no artist did more to rescue the river and press for its preservation as a majestic natural resource than Morgan Bulkeley. Words were his medium, the essay was his genre, and he was a master of the genre. For a dozen years, from 1960 until 1972, and sporadically thereafter, Bulkeley contributed essays to The Berkshire Eagle that appeared weekly under the heading "Our Berkshires." Altogether, he wrote more than 700 essays, several of which confronted readers with graphic evidence of the damage that thoughtless generations of Berkshirites had inflicted on the great river that flows through the county. Bulkeley became, in effect, the river's advocate and champion.

From the very start of his career as a columnist, Bulkeley revealed a prose style as clear and fresh as the air in the township of Mount Washington, where he lived and farmed during the early 1960s until failing eyesight prompted Morgan and his wife, Barbara, to move to Pittsfield.

At Yale, he had steeped himself in Emerson and Thoreau. As a postgraduate bachelor, he had ascended

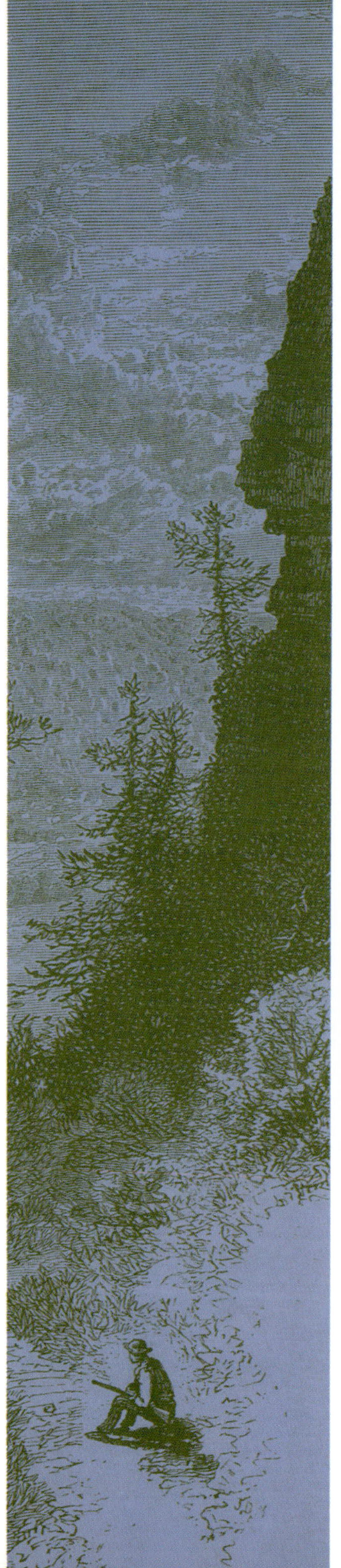

to Mount Washington where, following Thoreau's example, he had spent a year roughing it in a small cabin. As he informed readers in his introductory column, "I stayed the four seasons without spending more than a hundred dollars. I incurred no bills, there being no electricity, running water, automobile, radio, nor even a clock." He steeped himself in nature there, where, as he wrote, "the wildcat left his round footprint in the snow outside my window and the sound of flying squirrels playing over my roof was like rain in the night….And on a still, frosty night I could drift on the pond over the reflected stars, listening to the weird conversations of the owls."

In August of 1961, Bulkeley and an unnamed companion launched a canoe at the bridge on Holmes Road in Pittsfield to begin a two-day voyage down the Housatonic to Sheffield. After recalling that actress Fanny Kemble had thought the water of the river so pure that "it should be used only for baptism," Bulkeley writes:

> We did not find it thus….As the sun broke through over Canoe Meadows, the former Holmes property where Indian hunting parties once pulled out their birchbarks, it revealed an iridescent oil shimmer on the water. In many places the banks were graced by extensive beds of ostrich fern….But the tips were oil-blackened. Indeed, any vegetation at water level was coated with oil. The oil slick, sewage, and waste obviously repelled all wildlife in the river all the way down to Woods Pond at Lenox Station….There were no animal tracks on the fouled banks. Even birds seemed to shun the river.

In the third of three columns devoted to this exploratory voyage, Bulkeley was able to report that, as it distanced itself from industry, the river cleared progressively. That report, full of hope for the river, follows.

Bulkeley ended that voyage just below

Bartholomew's Cobble, another treasure he helped preserve, both as an essayist and as the energetic chairman of the Cobble Board during the 1960s. In 1975, by which time Bulkeley's eyesight was greatly impaired by glaucoma, he contributed a follow-up column titled "Headway on the Housatonic," in which he recounts what he had seen on the earlier voyage and goes on to provide a progress report. A succession of land acquisitions, some by gift and some purchase, he writes, has placed the remarkable total of approximately 1,150 acres along both banks of the Housatonic within the public domain in the last 12 years. He pays tribute to the massive volunteer participation in removing years of accumulated litter, rubbish, brush, and downed trees from the river and its banks, and goes on to observe:

> In the long view, the gradually destroyed Housatonic River in Berkshire County has been transformed from a dump and sewer into a growing, green park-corridor and a recreational resource. The change is perhaps best appreciated from the vantage point of the canoe, that primitive invention and original vessel of the Housatonic, that has somehow imparted the Indian's respect for the environment to his modern successor.

The graceful salute to the Indians, this stepping back for a moment into the past, is a typical touch of this master essayist who became the voice of the river and provided the impetus for its preservation and safekeeping.

Jon Swan is a poet, playwright, and freelance journalist who lives in New Marlborough.

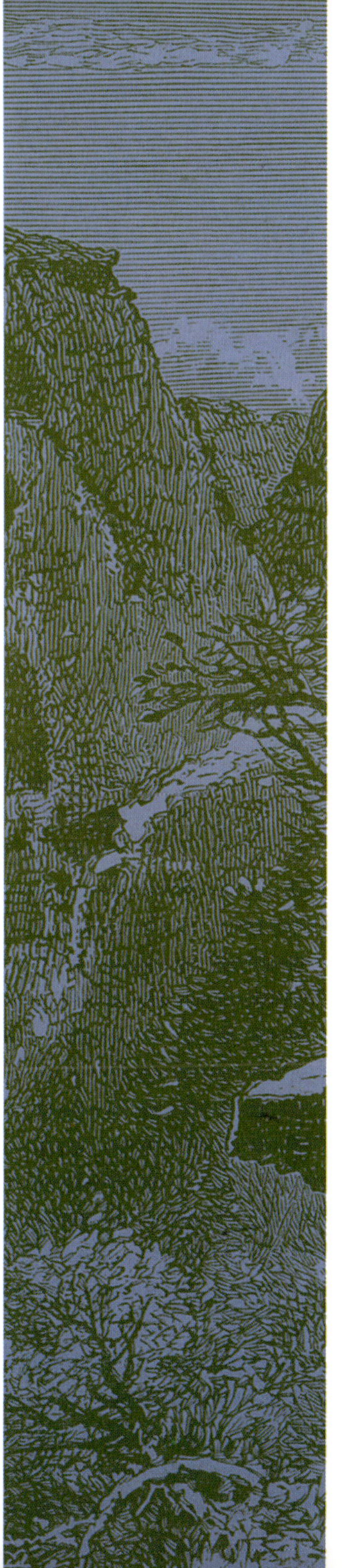

RIVER REPORT, AUGUST 1961

Morgan Bulkeley

Originally published in The Berkshire Eagle, August 24, 1961

In August of 1676, Major John Talcott was the first Englishman to see the Ausotunnoog River within Berkshire County. In an aftermath of King Philip's War, he pursued 200 Indian fugitives from the Valley over the Indian trail to the ford at the Great Wigwam, now the approximate site of Great Barrington. The name Housatonuk, meaning place-beyond-the-mountains, was first applied to this site, then to the Indians, and finally, to the entire river. Talcott's massacre of 25 Indians dabbled the bushes with blood and reddened the river. White men have been staining it ever since.

Into these dark waters at the ford we launched the canoe for the final tortuous course through the Sheffield Plain to the county line below Bartholomew's Cobble, a distance of 11.3 crow-flight miles and 22 canoe miles. As June Mountain fell back on the east, the broader, deeper river slithered its serpentine way through the wide plain dominated by Mount Everett on the west.

One twist after another showed the truth of Thoreau's observation: There is a male and female shore

to the river, one abrupt, the other flat and meadowy—
on the one hand eating into the bank, on the other
depositing sediment. Large trees were often toppled into
the river on the eroded side, creating a temporary
impasse for us and convenient shelter for wood ducks.

Around one bend we surprised a paddling of these
shy ducks in midstream. The young, not yet able to fly,
skittered over the surface to the protection of a snag
beside the bank, while the parent birds floundered
downriver barely ahead of us peeping anxiously, one
along each shore, using wings laboriously and
splashingly like broken paddle wheels. When their
stratagem had led us far enough downstream, they
arose effortlessly, if not derisively, and circled back
through the woods.

The water cleared progressively as we rode the lazy
current out onto the Sheffield Plain. The steep banks
became sandy, offering easy excavating to bank swallow,
kingfisher and muskrat. The latter often slid quietly into
the river ahead of us, leaving fresh diggings, caches of
clam shells, or simply a favored sunning spot. Painted
turtles slipped silently from logs ahead of us.

Around one bend we surprised a gaggle of two
dozen Canada geese on a gravel promontory, handsome
birds, yet inconspicuous with body feathering blending
into the pebbly background and a camouflage pattern
of black and white breaking up the head and neck
forms. The canoe drifted by like a lifeless log, and the
geese stalked off with stately gait into the tall grass.

The river, having learned of pollution at its origin,
after a flirtation with Route 7 recoiled east below the
covered bridges avoiding Sheffield and by twisting west

skirted Ashley Falls, thereby preserving a brown clarity that
must have been its color when Major Talcott first saw it.

Life in all forms was increasingly abundant. The
water surface was teeming in places with a new hatch
of some ephemera. The empty sarcophagi of dragonflies
clung to the sedges. Fish now and again broke the
surface, beneath which could be seen green water
plants. A great blue heron arose lazily from a sand bar
ahead, and we measured his huge footprints with our
hands that were smaller. We came upon two boys
catching rock bass while their grandfather dozed on
the grassy bank.

Below Bartholomew's Cobble approximately on
the state line, as if for a grace note at the end of our
trip, an American egret sprang from the water's edge
and lifted into the sunshine against a cumulus cloud
rendered dingy by comparison. His pure white was
somehow symbolic of a clean river.

Our two-day trip totaling 58 canoe miles from
Pittsfield to Weatogue showed the river at its worst and
at its best. There was certainly a measure of hope in the
fact that the down-county section seemed wild and
clean in spite of man's abuse upstream. This was no
passing languishing creature, but a sinuous beautiful
snake ready to slough off a scarred skin with the
assistance of the communities close to the bank. Here
was a living entity not irreparably damaged by past
misuse. In fact it seemed that one roaring spring flood
would be sufficient to purge it, if all defilement could
be stopped in the future.

Morgan Bulkeley, who recently turned 90, lives in Pittsfield.

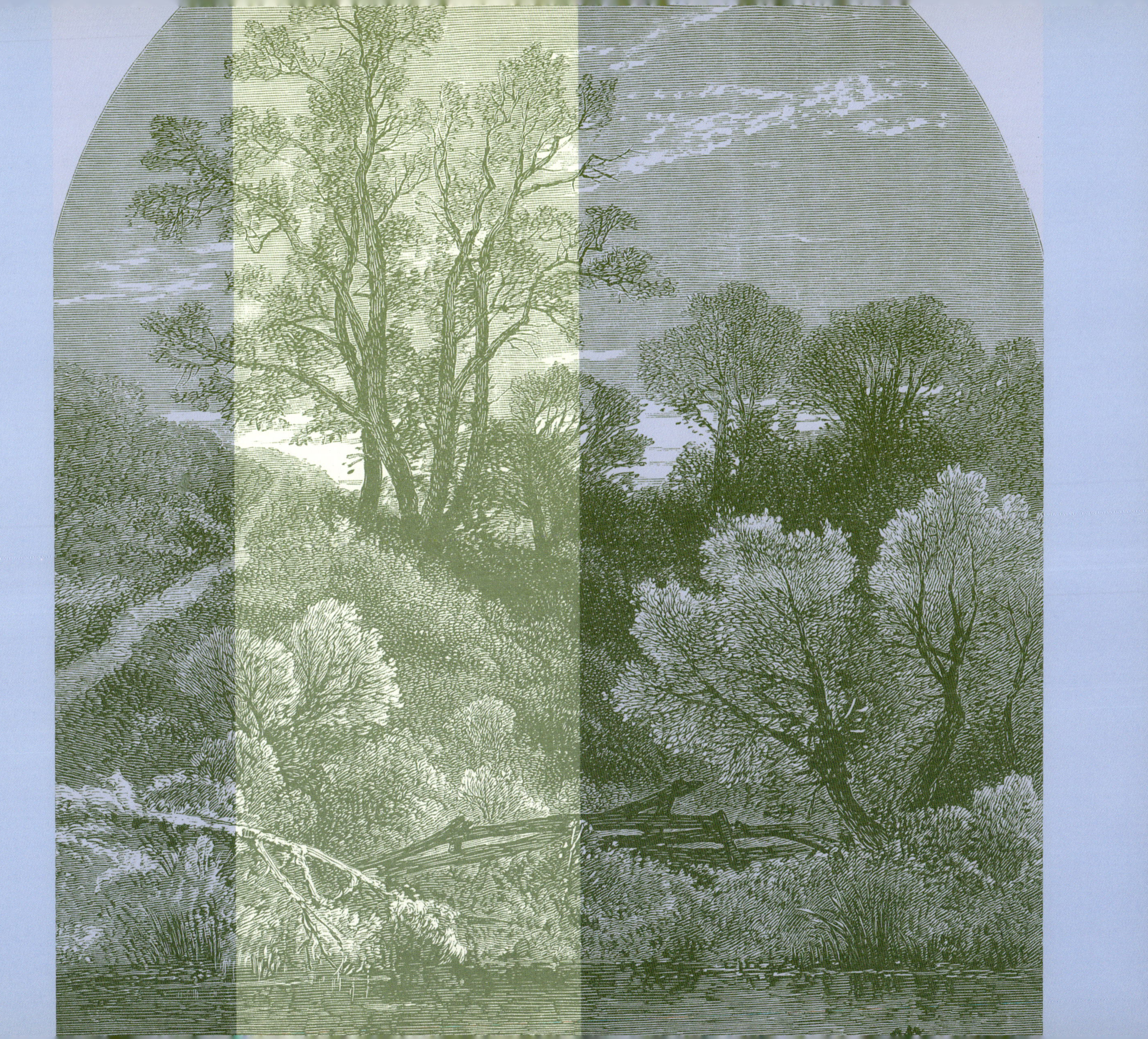

THE HOUSATONIC RUNS WILD

Liba H. Furhman

As the Housatonic leaves Massachusetts, passing south of Bartholomew's Cobble on its way to Long Island Sound, it takes on a new character. The river moves faster and faster through the rock ledges and hills of Connecticut's Northwest Corner, a scant two hours' drive from New York City, and becomes wild—and scenic—enough to have qualified, in the 1970s, for federal protection as a "wild and scenic river."

It's hard to imagine that just a century before that, these Housatonic reaches, home today to gentlemen farmers, historic covered bridges, some of the best trout fishing in the country, and the longest stretch of riverside Appalachian Trail, were an industrial landscape shaped by iron and the generation of electricity.

Bulls Bridge—one of the two remaining covered bridges that span the river in Connecticut—was built in 1781 by Jacob Bull to facilitate the transport of iron ore from New York state to a forge in Kent. From 1732 to 1923, dozens of blast furnaces operated in the Upper Housatonic Valley. According to some, the ironworks of the region were one reason the North won the Civil War. The Ames Ironworks, across the river from Falls Village, worked round the clock during the war, producing cannons capable of shooting a 50-pound

cannonball a distance of five miles. As the war drew to a close, the largest cannon in the world was built there, one capable of firing a 125-pound cannonball.

During the 1800s, the mountainsides near the river were laid bare, as hardwood trees were cut, piled in mounds, and slowly burned for weeks to produce the charcoal needed to fuel the furnaces. The lack of wood helped lead to the demise of the region's iron industry. Reforesting could not keep up with the demand for wood, and importing charcoal was too expensive. Today, many of the old charcoal pits can still be found in the forest, connected by remnants of old roads.

Starting in the 1840s, the Housatonic Railroad carried iron and other products of the region to market. Those included lime and limestone, marble, iron railcar wheels, coal, tobacco, and tools, as well as the valley's many agricultural products, including milk. The Housatonic was the first railroad in America to run a scheduled milk train, chugging from town to town to pick up hundreds of milk cans for shipment to New York City. The railroad also transported ice, cut from ponds and streams in winter, to chill both the milk and local customers' iceboxes.

From the earliest colonial days, the Housatonic River was a source of power. The first dams were built to operate gristmills and sawmills, then textile mills and paper mills. By the 1900s, the Connecticut portion of the river was being dammed to produce electricity.

The first large hydroelectric station in Connecticut—one of the first in the country—was built by the Housatonic Power Company just south of Kent, in New Milford. That Bulls Bridge plant, still in operation, went into service in 1903.

Two years later, J. Henry Roraback, a North Canaan lawyer and politician, planned a power system to supply the entire state. He organized the Rocky River Power Company, which in 1917 changed its name to the Connecticut Light and Power Company and acquired numerous power companies, including the Housatonic Power Company. Other hydropower facilities soon appeared on the river, including the Falls Village station, put into operation in 1914 and still running today. Built at the Great Falls of the Housatonic, the plant was admired both as a natural wonder and as a site of industrial accomplishment, realizing the full power of the falls.

Most towns up and down the Housatonic had factories along its banks and used the river as both a source of water for their manufacturing or milling processes and a dumping ground for their waste products. Trash and sewage thrown in the river exceeded the river's capacity to assimilate waste. Gone were most of the natural waterfalls and rapids, lost when the dams were built. For much of the time now, the Great Falls, which had a drop greater than 90 feet in the early nineteenth century, has no water because the flow is diverted to the power plant.

All this changed the way people thought about the river.

That the Connecticut portion of the river is as wild and scenic as it is today is largely thanks to Dr. Charles Downing Lay, noted landscape architect, Yale University professor, and passionate conservationist. He had a home in Stratford, at the mouth of the Housatonic River, and a camp on Cornwall's Coltsfoot Mountain. It was he who in the 1930s sounded the alarm.

Afraid that development and growth would destroy his beloved river valley, he knew that the valley needed to be looked at as a whole, not just town by town, and that choices had to be made. Where and how growth should occur, what we might lose or choose to save, how to restore a majestic river and safeguard its pastoral and wooded valley lands—these are the questions he explored.

Slowly but surely, others in the Northwest Corner came to see that Lay was right. In 1940, the town of

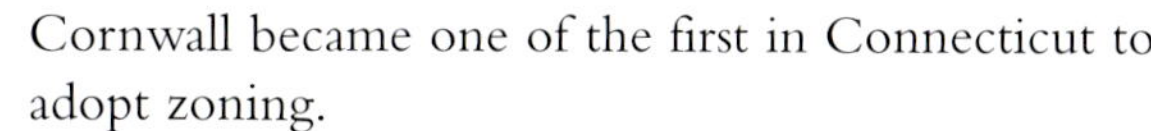

Cornwall became one of the first in Connecticut to adopt zoning.

Lay was tireless. He composed countless articles and letters to legislators and newspaper editors arousing public awareness and promoting land-use reform. In 1941, he called an open meeting in Falls Village and there was born the Housatonic Valley Conference (today known as the Housatonic Valley Association), the first watershed conservation group in the nation. His goal was ambitious: to restore and conserve the beauty of the river by pressing for zoning codes that would provide for industry-free scenic river corridors and residential setbacks.

By the 1970s, on the wave of public awakening about environmental issues, the Housatonic once again became the focus of concern. Area activists like Cornwall's Monty Hare carried on Lay's philosophy of looking at the entire river watershed as one. "The river is everywhere the same river, and so long as any part of it is polluted, the whole of it is," he wrote in 1973. And Hare matter-of-factly predicted, "To clean up our waters, our land and air, is of course going to cost a lot of money."

Following the discovery of PCB contamination downstream from a General Electric facility on the Hudson River, the Housatonic Valley Association performed the first tests for PCBs in the Connecticut section of the Housatonic. The tests did reveal PCBs, forcing the Connecticut Department of Environmental Protection and the U.S. Environmental Protection Agency to acknowledge the problem in this river as well.

The '70s also saw a new era of protection through government action. With new federal legislation—the Water Pollution Control Act and the Clean Water Act— a system for controlling river pollution by mandating removal of chemicals from wastewater discharged into rivers was established.

In 1979, a U.S. Department of the Interior study

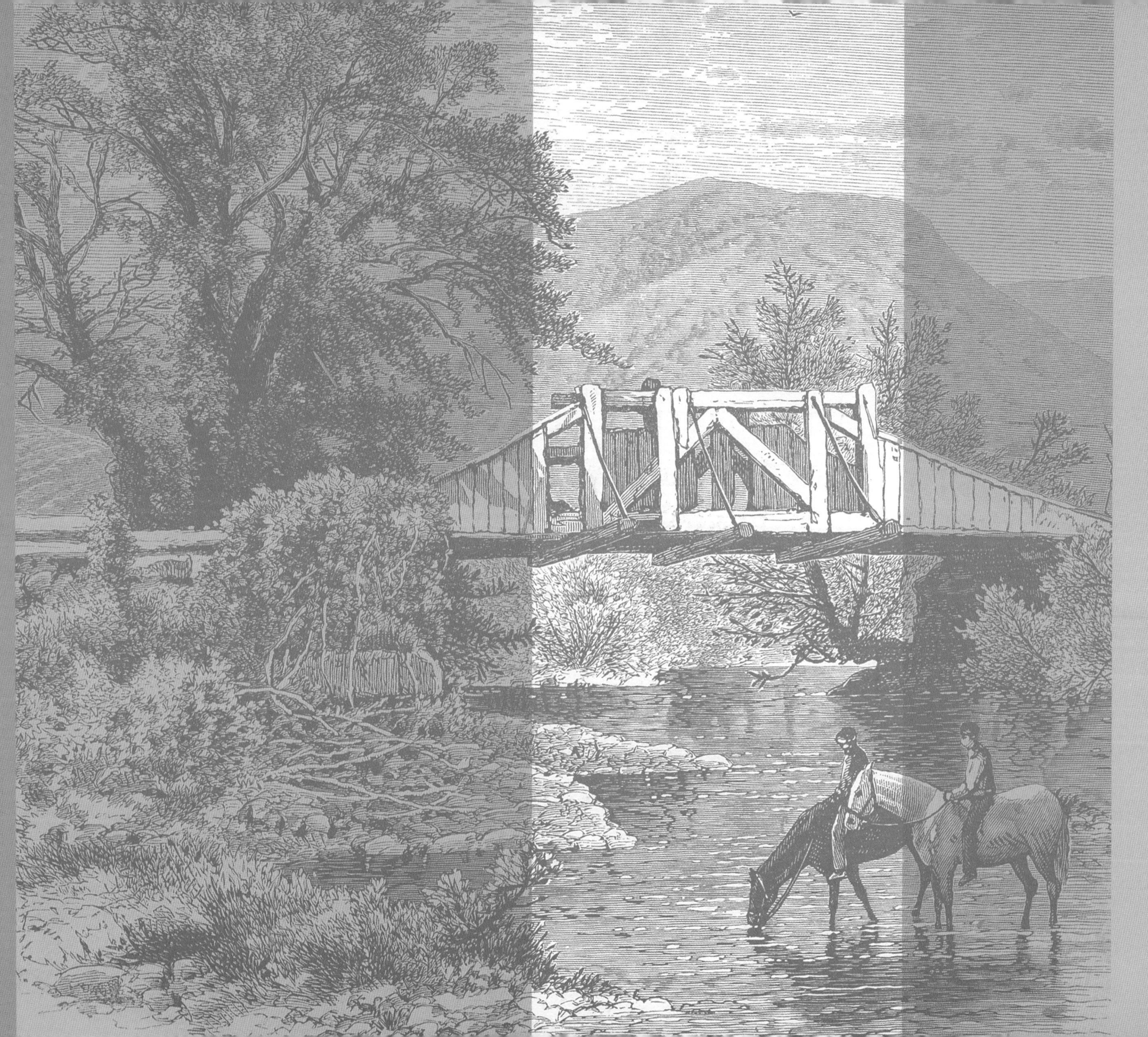

qualified the Housatonic River between the Massachusetts border and Boardman Bridge in New Milford for protection under the National Wild and Scenic Rivers Act. Riverside communities, however, opted for local protection and established the Housatonic River Commission, which drafted a river management plan and advises on projects related to the river's protection and development.

The valley's strategic location has led to other kinds of threats to the river. In the 1970s, the Housatonic Valley Association, the Housatonic River Watershed Association of Western Massachusetts, and other groups fought the building of a superhighway through the Northwest Corner and the Berkshires.

In the 1980s, citizens again banded together, this time to minimize the impact of a natural gas pipeline that would cut a swath from Canada to Long Island. The original route ran through Salisbury, Sharon, Kent, and 15 other valley towns—and through conservation lands, wetlands, and protected open space, crossing the river three times. Under the leadership of HVA's Lynn Werner, citizens attended hearings and meetings to urge federal regulators to deny the route. In partnership with the Berkshire-Litchfield Environmental Council and dozens of environmental groups like the Washington Environmental Council, Steep Rock Association, Stop the Pipe, and The Weantinoge Heritage, arguments for using existing rights-of-way eventually won out. The Iroquois Gas Transmission System changed its proposal away from sensitive landscapes, and the final route avoided two river crossings, along with many wetland systems, sensitive ridgelines, and other natural treasures.

That same decade, the National Park Service, together with the Housatonic Valley Association, Joseph Hickey from the Connecticut Department of Environmental Protection, and community leaders from the towns of Kent, Cornwall, and Sharon, hammered

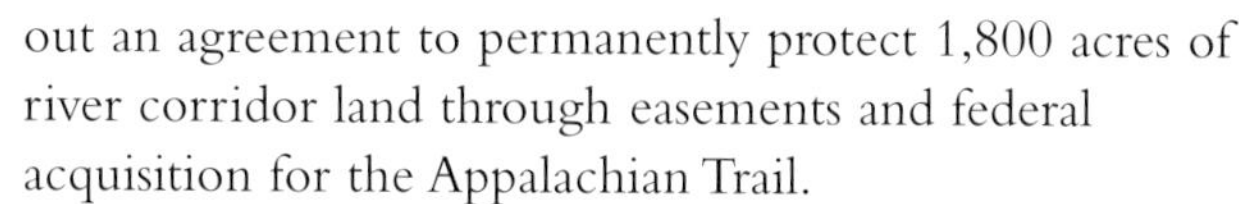

out an agreement to permanently protect 1,800 acres of river corridor land through easements and federal acquisition for the Appalachian Trail.

Today, threats to the Connecticut portion of the river come mainly from the pressures of development. The population of the region has grown dramatically over the past 20 years, bringing an increased demand for riverfront and recreational use. Run-off from residential and commercial development—fertilizers and pesticides, road sand, salt, and oil—is the single worst source of new pollution for the Housatonic River.

Large swaths of open meadow and forest are being fragmented, eliminating important wildlife habitat. In some parts of the region, rural landscapes are being converted to suburban and urban uses at a rate of five square miles each year. The window of opportunity for preserving the character of Connecticut's Northwest Corner is small, and closing. Large tracts of forest and farmland—and all that is sustained by them—could be lost within 25 years.

As we moved into the new century, Northeast Utilities, the largest single private landowner along the Housatonic River, was poised to be acquired by Consolidated Edison, raising fears that the company would divest itself of its land assets along the river, bringing development throughout the valley. Working with the company, the state, and other environmental groups, the Housatonic Valley Association negotiated a ten-year moratorium on any sale and is now working with towns and land trusts to permanently protect these lands.

Currently, the Federal Energy Regulatory Commission is reviewing applications for renewal of the license to operate the Falls Village, Bulls Bridge, and other Northeast Generating hydropower plants. Fishing clubs and environmental groups are urging that any new license require that more natural water flows be restored for fish and aquatic life and provide for protection of riverside open space as well.

GE's settlement with the EPA has required it to dredge portions of the river in Massachusetts and provide an $8-million restoration fund. The Connecticut Trustee Advisory Group and its counterpart in Massachusetts are planning for efforts such as improving water quality and fishery resources, along with improving access to the river and building trails and bikeways. The advisory groups represent a wide spectrum of river interests.

Citizen efforts continue to maintain the beauty and natural diversity of the river ecosystem through many programs. Every year, more riverfront land is permanently protected, adding more and more miles to the Housatonic Valley Association's Housatonic River Belt Greenway. Connecticut "stream team" volunteers work with Ruth Malins to assess river conditions and water quality. Others, like Norm Sills of the Connecticut Chapter of the Appalachian Mountain Club's Trails Committee, help to provide public access to the river. Yet others, like Elaine LaBella, HVA's land protection director, involve themselves in the political and regulatory process to ensure a clean and healthy river for all. Sharon historian Ed Kirby preserves the records and remnants of the early iron days through his writings, photographic records, and restoration work of the Beckley Furnace. And the Housatonic River Commission's Cilla Mauro and Lynn Fowler head up a yearly River Appreciation Day for area students

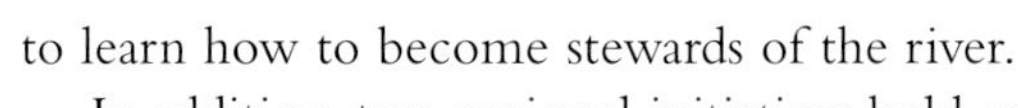

to learn how to become stewards of the river.

In addition, two regional initiatives hold great promise for the future of the Housatonic River:

• A National Park Service National Heritage Area is being proposed for the Upper Housatonic Valley. The study, with Lakeville's Ron Jones as chairman, proposes to preserve natural and historic resources, encourage low-impact economic development, control undesirable growth, and promote the continuing cleanup of the river.

• The Highlands Coalition, consisting of more than 100 state, local, and environmental groups from Pennsylvania to Connecticut, recognizes the special characteristics of Connecticut's Northwest Corner and is working to protect and connect recognized "critical treasures" and to ensure smart and sustainable growth. HVA Executive Director Lynn Werner, in partnership with Tim Northrop of the Trust for Public Lands, is leading the effort in Connecticut.

Today, Charles Lay would be pleased to see what has been accomplished since his open meeting in Falls Village—that the river he loved runs wild again. He would know, too, that some of the greatest challenges to preserve and protect the resources and heritage of the Housatonic River Valley lie ahead.

Liba H. Furhman is the director of community affairs for the Housatonic Valley Association. A former mayor of New Milford, Connecticut, she has long been an environmental grassroots activist.

WE ARE ALL RIVER STEWARDS

Rachel Fletcher

He who knows his Berkshire will never omit the praise of the Housatonic…the stream which like a silver cord binds the scenes of Berkshire into one volume.
—John Coleman Adams,
"Nature Studies in Berkshire," 1901

Its waters collect from as high as the peak of Mount Greylock and as low as the Sheffield flats. It flows through great geologic formations of limestone, marble, and schist, through dark woodland forests, rich floodplain soils, and shallow marshes. I know the Housatonic by its flowers, from the first blush of shadbush to the last stand of purple asters that survive the chill of fall. I know the spring by vernal pools and the unmistakable clamor of peepers. I know summer by the ferns that green its banks. In autumn, the river sparks metallic, reflecting golden sugar maples and the deep steel blue of sky. And I know it is winter by the dark and brooding power that flows past icy sheets.

Long after the Native American Mohicans settled the Housatonic River Valley, the Housatonic became a working river, as early European settlements became cities and towns, and modest gristmills grew into paper and textile mills, and ultimately into modern industrial plants. It was a time of denial, as communities built

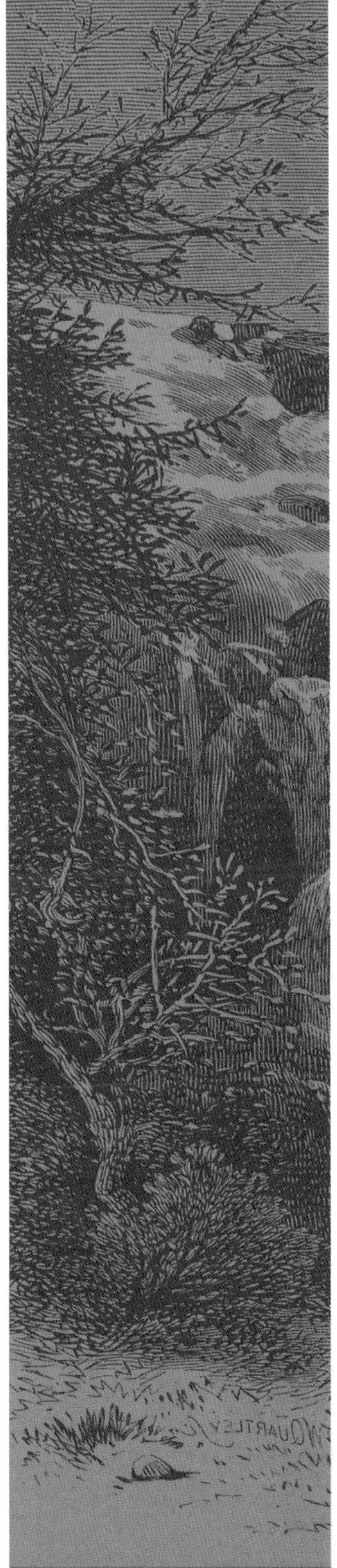

their towns with backs to the river, and the river fell prey to abuse and discarded waste.

In the nineteenth century, writers and artists—Frederick Edwin Church, William Cullen Bryant, Thomas Cole, to name a few—managed to see through to the river's essential beauty. At the turn of the twentieth century, John Coleman Adams, a Universalist minister, raised the alarm:

> The hour in which the modern man settles beside a river is a bad one for the stream….He tries to tire it out with work, to exhaust it with cruelties. He strangles it with dams, and poisons it with dye-stuffs, and chokes it with sewage, and stifles it in steam-boilers. He tries to starve it to death by cutting off the forest on the mountains which it feeds itself. He sedulously kills all the fish between its banks. And still the river forgives all and tries its best to keep up the struggle for existence….Here in our Housatonic is a noble example of how hard a river dies.

Today the Housatonic is winding back into the hearts of our towns and communities, in a story of stewardship and renewal. We owe much to the visions and warnings of these early artists and writers, the first to shed light on a river cursed by neglect.

> Rescue the Housatonic and clean it as we have never in all the years thought before of cleaning it…restore its ancient beauty; making it the center of a town, of a valley, and perhaps—who knows?—of a new measure of civilized life.
> —W. E. B. Du Bois, 1930

Another early advocate for the river was Great Barrington native William E. B. Du Bois, the father of Pan-Africanism and champion of American civil rights. "I was born by a golden river," he wrote, and he campaigned for its recovery throughout his life. In the 1930s, he called on the town to stop treating the river like a sewer and instead to envision a time when "parks and boulevards would line the redeemed river; when canoes and pleasure boats and swimming children would make the whole valley glad and the river would come into its own again."

His was a radical vision that tied the fate of the river to environmental justice, social responsibility, and human rights. He embraced every river landscape, even the discarded and abused, and imagined people of all races and vocations—workers, artists, farmers, naturalists and children—coming to the aid of the river, to shape its destiny as well as their own:

> For this valley, the river must be the center. Certainly it is the physical center; perhaps, in a sense, the spiritual center. Perhaps from that very freeing of spirit will come other freedoms and inspirations and aspirations which may be steps toward the diffusion and diversification and enriching of culture throughout this land.

Adams and Du Bois might be pleased that bands of local citizens today are tackling river cleanups and restorations, transforming their pride in manual labor into a new ecological code of conduct. In the late 1980s, a contingent of 12 local residents undertook the daunting task of clearing the remains of a burned-out building from the banks of the Housatonic in downtown Great Barrington. Since then, 1,900 volunteers have come from near and far to reclaim and transform the town's once ravished riverbank, removing 360 tons of rubble and waste and restoring native habitat. A half-mile of handcrafted trail and wetland gardens now meanders along the river's edge where Du Bois once envisioned his boulevards and parks. One may enter the trail at Church Street through the Du Bois River Garden, just steps away from where he was born.

Ordinary citizens who work to remove debris may recover the artifacts of history. They confront the abuses of industry in mounds of mass-produced plastics and

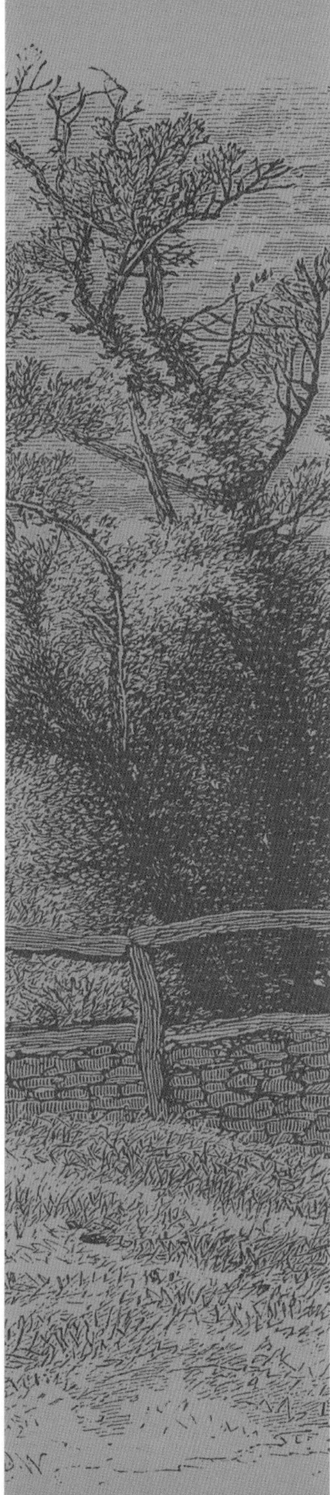

metals. They renew lost ties to native cultures when they find a deftly wrought spearpoint of churt. Memories of a rich and complex history of human use come to light through simple acts of caretaking. New memories are created and these, too, are laid into the soil, as by a laying-on of hands. Like so much of our New England landscape, the beauty that results is more handcrafted than wild.

When cities and towns reclaim abandoned rivers, a rich historical and natural heritage is revealed underfoot. There is a new regard for wildlife habitat, native flora, vistas and views, avenues of transport, geological formations, wetland and floodplain ecology, historic and prehistoric patterns of human settlement, and local legend. Rivers are places of confluence where culture and nature meet, and cannot be separated from the people who live by them.

Throughout the Housatonic River Valley, volunteers are restoring the landscape, creating buffers of native plants to absorb agricultural runoff, and growing gardens of wetland flowers to treat storm water from rooftops and streets. Some watch over the river, measuring its quality and flow to document its condition. Others build greenways and trails. It is still not advisable to swim in the Housatonic, nor eat what is caught in its waters. But on any given day, families stroll along walkways; fishermen catch and release; sportsmen kayak and canoe; painters set up their easels; and increasing numbers of children learn about their world by playing in nature's schoolroom.

The river belongs to all of us. We are all responsible for its future. We are all river stewards, and we are taking the river back.

Rachel Fletcher has lived in Great Barrington for 23 years. She is the founding director of the town's Housatonic River Walk, executive director of Housatonic River Restoration, and owner of Foggy River Farm on the Williams River.

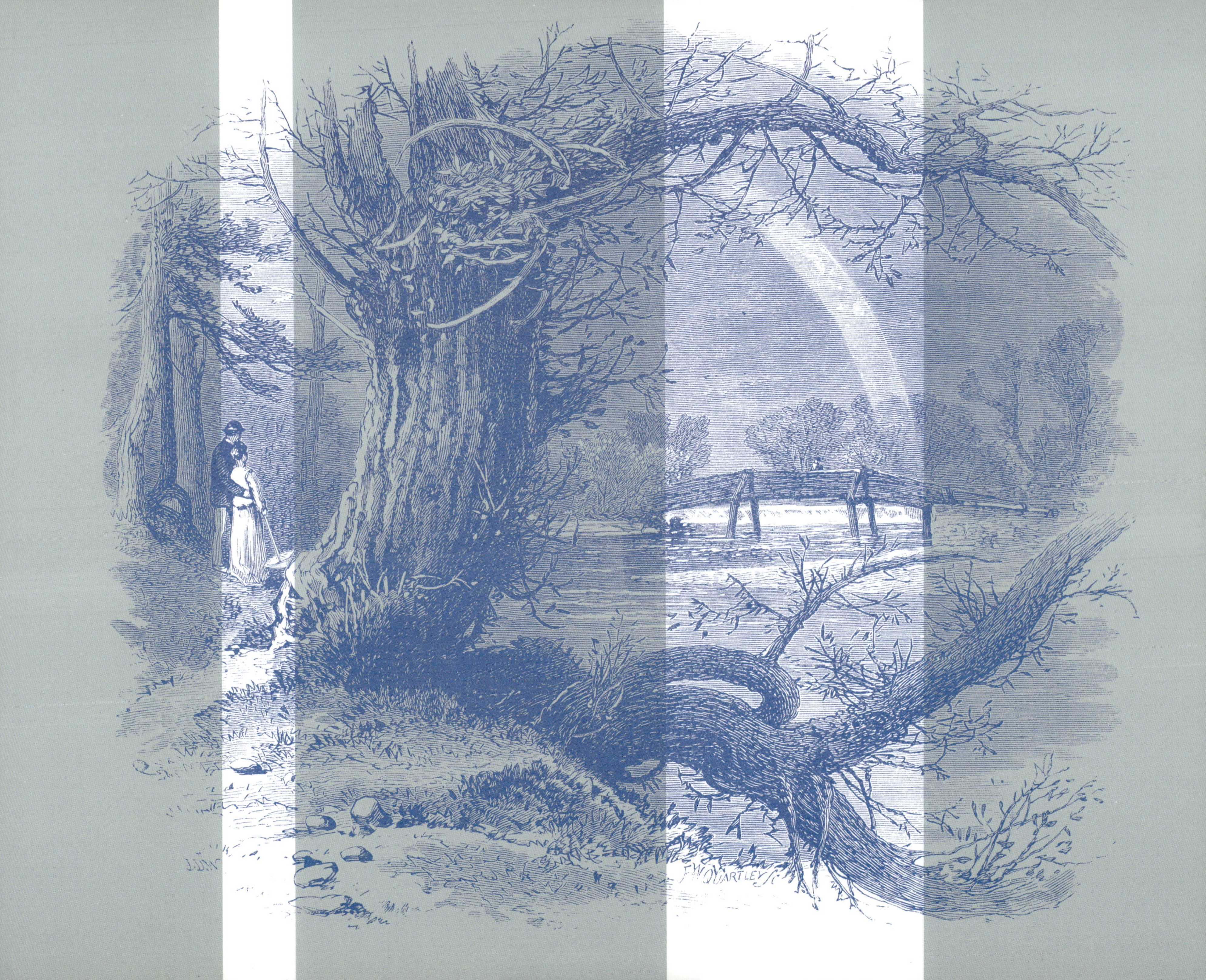

J. D. N.
F. W. QUARTLEY sc.

BIOGRAPHIES

Historical Artists

William Cullen Bryant, nineteenth-century writer and poet, left for posterity one of the most charming collections of images of the way America used to look in the era of romanticism. His two-volume "Picturesque America or The Land We Live In," first published in 1874 by D. Appleton and Company in New York, is an extraordinary compendium of essays and etchings by prominent American artists of the mountains, rivers, lakes, forests, waterfalls, shores, valleys, cities, and other picturesque features of our country. Several of the etchings from the chapter "Valley of the Housatonic," written by W. C. Richards, are reproduced in this book.

Thomas Cole (1801-1848), whose art laid the foundation for what would emerge as the Hudson River School of landscape painters, was apparently the first professional landscape artist to work in the Berkshires. In 1833, on his way from Albany to Boston, Cole visited Pittsfield and made drawings of Pontoosuc Lake. He finished a painting (shown in this book) in his New York studio of Mount Greylock, known at the time as Hoosac Mountain. Cole was a close friend of William Cullen Bryant who, after Cole's death, delivered a memorial address before the New York Historical Society.

Edward Gay (1837-1928), born in Ireland, came to America with his parents in the wake of the Potato Famine. As a young man he returned to Europe to study art in Germany. When he returned to the U.S. in 1864, landscape painting was in vogue. With his wife, he moved to Mount Vernon, New York, and made frequent trips to northwestern Connecticut to paint. Gay was made an Associate of the National Academy in 1868, the same year he painted the Twin Lakes view that is reproduced in this book. His works are in many museum and library collections.

Hobart Nichols (1869-1962) was a regular visitor to his brother Spencer's studio in Kent, Connecticut. He practiced a vigorous form of impressionism and is closely identified with the New England landscape, especially in snow. Nichols attended the Art Students League in Washington, D.C., and later the Academie Julian in France. He was the recipient of innumerable awards, including the Altman Prize, which he won an unprecedented three times. He was elected a National Academician in 1920 and served as president of the Academy from 1939 to 1949. He is the uncle of Helen Nichols Jacobs, whose work is shown in the Contemporary Artists section of this book.

Arthur Parton (1842-1914), a specialist in rendering streams and rivers, worked principally in the summer months in the Adirondacks and Catskills, but visited the Berkshires as well. He learned how to paint water as a student at the Philadelphia Academy of Fine Arts, along with learning about the Hudson River School and the Pre-Raphaelites. Although he produced his large canvases in his New York studio, Parton was praised for his ability to communicate the experience of being outdoors. He was a regular exhibitor at the National Academy of Design in New York. His works are represented at the Metropolitan Museum of Art.

Anthon Henry Wenzler (?-1871), also known as Henry Antonio Wenzler, was a Danish native who moved to the U.S. at an early age. He was known for his portraits, landscapes, and still lifes. Although he was active as a painter in New York City and was a member of the National Academy, he evidently also spent time in Connecticut and Massachusetts. He completed paintings of the Great Falls in Falls Village, Connecticut, as well as a view of Great Barrington (shown in this book).

Contemporary Artists

Morgan Bulkeley, Jr., grew up in Mount Washington in the southern Berkshires, son of Morgan Bulkeley, the naturalist and journalist whose essays about the plight of the Housatonic River served as an early warning in the community. As a boy, Morgan, Jr., roamed through the woods and creeks around his home, befriending birds and wild animals. As an artist, he features these creatures in oil paintings and sculptures that have been described as narrative and primitive. Bulkeley has shown his work extensively across the nation, in New York, Boston, Florida, California, and Chicago. Many of his paintings and sculptures are in private and corporate collections as well as museums. He is currently represented by the Geoffrey Young Gallery in Great Barrington, Massachusetts, and the Howard Yezerski Gallery in Boston.

Emily Buchanan is a plein air painter who studied primarily in the atelier of Boston School painter Paul Ingbretson. A resident of West Cornwall, Connecticut, she is known for her Connecticut landscapes and coastal scenes of Massachusetts and the islands. Buchanan's work has been exhibited broadly in solo and group shows in New England, New York, Atlanta, and London. She is currently represented by Holland & Co. in Bedford, New York; the Gardner-Colby Gallery in Martha's Vineyard and Naples, Florida; Morgan Lehman in Lakeville, Connecticut; and Jane Deering in London.

Bart Elsbach, a resident of Sheffield, Massachusetts, explores the landscape around him and its effects within. His haunting images vary in their emphasis on direct visual cues and internal musings. He received his MFA at New York University in New York City and was also educated at the Art Students League. Elsbach has had numerous one-person shows since the mid-1980s in New York and New England. In collections throughout the U.S. and abroad, he currently exhibits at O.K. Harris in New York; Leslie Ferrin in Lenox, Massachusetts; David Klein in Birmingham, Michigan; and The Doran Gallery in Tulsa, Oklahoma.

Frank Federico, a seasoned artist in many media as well as a popular and compassionate teacher, lives in Goshen, Connecticut. He has been painting the Housatonic River for over 20 years. He is a Master Pastelist with the Pastel Society of America. His work has met with enthusiasm by collectors and critics around the world. Federico has received dozens of major awards from a broad spectrum of artists' organizations. One of his murals hangs in the Student Union of the University of Connecticut in Storrs. He was recently honored by a major retrospective at the West Hartford Art League. Federico is an honorary member of the Sheffield Art League and one of its most popular teachers.

Warner Friedman is known for his unusual interpretations of landscapes as seen through stationary architectonic structures. As stated in a recent catalogue of his show at the Boca Raton Museum of Art, Friedman's art reflects "the impulse to breathe in an unbreathable world." He has been the recipient of a number of foundation grants and fellowships. His work has been shown in numerous one-person and group exhibitions in galleries, universities, and museums from the Berkshires and Connecticut to New York, Pennsylvania, Florida, Arizona, and Texas. His works are also in public and private collections. A transplanted New Yorker, Friedman has lived in Sheffield, Massachusetts, for the past 25 years.

Ann Getsinger's formal art training includes Paier School of Art (1975) and The San Francisco Art Institute (1979). Born in Connecticut not far from the Housatonic River, Getsinger has lived in the Berkshires for some 25 years, with a home and studio in New Marlborough since 1988. She works in oils, in a realist style, with a wide range of favorite subjects. Her work is in many private collections. She has had a number of one-person shows and, in 1998, received an Artists' Resource Trust Grant. Her work can be seen locally at Tokonoma Gallery in Housatonic.

Arshile Gorky (1904-1948), the Abstract Expressionist painter, arrived in the United States from Armenia about 1920 and taught at the New School of Design in Boston. In 1925 he moved to New York and entered the Grand Central School of Art in New York as a student, but soon became an instructor. Throughout the 1920s, Gorky's painting was influenced by Georges Braque, Paul Cézanne, and, above all, Pablo Picasso. In 1930 Gorky's work was included in a group show at the Museum of Modern Art in New York. His first solo show took place at the Mellon Galleries in Philadelphia in 1931. In the mid '30s, he worked under the WPA Federal Art Project on murals for Newark Airport. From 1942 to 1948, he worked for part of each year in the countryside of Connecticut or Virginia. A succession of personal tragedies, including a fire in his studio that destroyed much of his work, a serious operation, and an automobile accident, preceded Gorky's death by suicide on July 21, 1948, in Sherman, Connecticut. He was recently given a retrospective at the Whitney Museum of Art in New York City.

Joan Griswold is known primarily for her paintings of interiors and streetscapes. As a teenager, Griswold lived in Japan for four years with her family and later studied painting at Beloit College in Wisconsin. Griswold continued her studies in Paris before moving to New York City, where she owned and operated a frame shop and art gallery. She has lived in the Berkshires since 1986 and works in her studio in Great Barrington, where she also teaches painting. She is represented by Hoorn-Ashby Gallery in New York City and Nantucket, Massachusetts, and the Hoadley Gallery in Lenox, Massachusetts. Her work is in many private and public collections.

Helen Nichols Jacobs grew up in the world of art and artists. She was born in Kent, Connecticut, the daughter of the artist Spencer B. Nichols, the granddaughter of Henry Hobart Nichols, a wood engraver, and niece of Hobart Nichols, a Bronxville, New York, artist who visited his brother in Kent frequently. A long-standing member of the Kent Art Association, as well as the Ridgewood (New Jersey) Art

Association, where she taught for more than 25 years, Jacobs has had her work in numerous shows in New England, New Jersey, and notably at the Winter Olympics in Nagano, Japan. Her work is in several corporate and private collections, and she's listed in "Who's Who in American Art." Jacobs lives in Paramus, New Jersey.

Donald Jurney studied at New York's Art Students League and at the Pratt Institute in Brooklyn. A Berkshire resident since 1986, he lived on a farm along the Housatonic River, in Sheffield, Massachusetts, from 1991 to 1999. His paintings are in a number of museum and corporate collections, both in the U.S. and abroad. In recent years, his work has concentrated on the French countryside. He currently lives in France and Virginia. Jurney is listed in "Who's Who in American Art." His work is represented by Hoorn-Ashby Gallery in New York City and Nantucket, Massachusetts.

John Manikowski, outdoorsman, cook, and wildlife and landscape artist, earned an MA from Rhode Island School of Design and taught in the Masters of Art in Teaching program at Harvard University. He came to the Berkshires in 1972 as a recipient of a National Endowment Grant to be artist-in-residence at Monument Mountain High School in Great Barrington. He has remained in the town of Mill River ever since. He has exhibited in over 25 galleries and exhibitions, in New York City and across the United States. His work is in private and public collections. Manikowski has illustrated several nature books, written and illustrated for magazines such as Field and Stream, and authored and illustrated two of his own cookbooks. His work is represented by Holland and Holland in New York City.

David McCandless was born in Great Barrington, Massachusetts, and remembers family stories about the Housatonic River. He was trained as an architect and lived for many years in Austin, Texas, before moving back to Great Barrington. His art career began with the study of watercolors. He joined and later became a signature member in the Southwestern Watercolor Society in Dallas and the Texas Watercolor Society in San Antonio, winning prizes in juried shows. He has been painting full-time, almost exclusively in pastels, since his retirement almost 15 years ago. He is an active member of the Sheffield Art League, teaching workshops on perspective in art, and has been a member of the League's board since 1999.

George L. K. Morris (1905-1975), a prominent American Abstractionist in the 1930s and 1940s, grew up in the Berkshires on a bucolic estate straddling the border of Lenox and Stockbridge. After studying in Paris with Fernand Leger and being introduced to the cubist movement, Morris returned to America to paint. Pursuing the ideal of pure abstraction, he embraced historically American subject matter with the new modern language of art. Some of his paintings of the Berkshire area, including *Housatonic River,* reproduced in this book, reflect his affection for the region and the legacy of the relationship between the European settlers and Native Americans. In 1930, he built an International-style studio, and later a house, on the 47 acres of land he inherited from his family. These buildings and grounds are now open to the public as the Frelinghuysen Morris House and Studio.

Geoffrey Moss works as a painter, teacher, writer and illustrator of children's books, set designer, and photographer/author of "The Biker Code," his newest book about America's edgy motorcycle culture. His work has been represented through museums including the Museum of Modern Art and the Berkshire Museum, as well as in galleries and corporate collections. Most recently, his work was exhibited as part of "In the Spirit of Martin" at the Smithsonian Institution in Washington, DC, and seven other museums. A political satirist twice nominated for the Pulitzer Prize, he is creator of "Mossprints," a syndicated visual column recognized as an artist's take on the world. Moss is currently represented in the Berkshires by the Lenox Gallery of Fine Art. He maintains studios in Alford, Massachusetts, and New York City and holds degrees from the University of Vermont and the Yale School of Art & Architecture.

Woldemar Neufeld (1909-2002) was born in Russia. He fled with his mother and stepfather, a Mennonite bishop, to Canada after his father's political execution in 1920. Neufeld's education as an artist took place in Canada and later Cleveland, as part of the Ash Can school. He settled in New York City, becoming known as Artist Laureate of the East River, and summered in Connecticut, ultimately settling there year-round. Neufeld's work hangs in many private collections and public museums and galleries. He decided to celebrate his adopted country's bicentennial by painting all 65 of the bridges crossing the Housatonic, from Hinsdale in Massachusetts to Stratford on Long Island Sound. Several of these paintings hang at the Cornwall Bridge headquarters of the Housatonic Valley Association.

June Parker's luminous pastels of the Berkshire landscape have earned a host of major awards in a number of different venues, including the Academic Art Association, Connecticut Pastel Society, the Hudson Valley Art Association, the Pastel Society of America, and the New Britain Museum of American Art. Parker is known for her commissioned work of portraits, private homes, and landmark buildings. Her work is in private and corporate collections in the U.S., Canada, Europe, and Australia. She is listed in the 2003-2004 edition of "Who's Who in American Art." A long-time art teacher and member of the Sheffield Art League, Parker's work can be seen in her own Gallery on the Green in South Egremont, Massachusetts, where she makes her home.

Erica Child Prud'homme's work is most often based on natural forms. She is known in particular for drawings and paintings of the human figure transposed as landscape. Prud'homme lives and has studios in both New York City and West Cornwall, Connecticut, where she has done illustrations for The Cornwall Chronicle and the town report. She studied art with her father, the painter Charles Child, with Anna Walinska, and at the Art Students League in New York City. She has worked as an architectural draftsman and as an exhibition designer at the American Museum of Natural History. She exhibits at the Blue Mountain Gallery in New York City and at various galleries in Massachusetts, Rhode Island, and Connecticut. Her most recent exhibit, in 2003 at the Cornwall Arts Collection, was "Housatonic River Paintings."

Jim Schantz received his Masters in Painting at University of California, Davis, and his BFA at Syracuse University. He also studied at the Hornsey School of Art in London and at the Skowhegan School in Maine. His works are in numerous public collections. Schantz has had six solo exhibitions at the Pucker Gallery in Boston and has been featured in exhibitions at the Berkshire Museum, the Springfield Museum of Fine Arts, the Albany Institute of Art, and the Brooklyn Museum. His book "Spirit of Nature: The Berkshire Landscapes of Jim Schantz" represents nearly a decade of work. Pucker Gallery recently released "Places of the Spirit: Music and Images Inspired by the Berkshires" with music by the renowned flutist Paula Robison and images by Jim Schantz. He lives in Glendale, Massachusetts.

Gabrielle Senza has been a center of energy in the Berkshire art world for over a decade. As owner and director of the former SPAZI Contemporary Art in Housatonic, Massachusetts, she curated and organized years of shows of prominent contemporary artists, photographers, writers, and performance artists. She has received awards for her own work and been exhibited widely in solo and group exhibitions in the U.S., Cuba, and Italy. Her art is in private, corporate, and public collections, including the Whitney and the Museum of Modern Art. In addition to painting, Senza is now teaching, writing, and heading up a non-profit arts initiative called Red Collaborative. She lives in North Egremont, Massachusetts.

Mary Sipp-Green has been working for the past 20 years as a landscape painter in the Berkshires. Her shimmering and poetic exploration of the contact points of water, land, and sky distinguishes her work. Her work has been included in books on new American art, has graced the covers of CDs, and is in private and public collections. She is currently represented by the Arden Gallery in Boston, Ganary Gallery in Martha's Vineyard, and Multiple Impressions in New York. Green lives in the Interlaken section of Stockbridge, Massachusetts.

Margot Trout was educated at the Rhode Island School of Design, where she received a BFA in painting. She also holds an MFA in art education from Hunter College and an MFA in painting from the University of Massachusetts. A long-time teacher of art, she is now retired, living in Great Barrington, Massachusetts, and painting full-time. Trout's Berkshire landscapes have been widely exhibited in Maine, Massachusetts, and New York. She has had two museum exhibitions and several one-person shows, and her prize-winning paintings are in many private collections. She is currently represented by the Lenox Gallery of Fine Art in Lenox, Massachusetts; the Stowe Art Gallery in Stowe, Vermont; and Alpers Fine Art in Andover, Massachusetts. Two of her paintings hang in the Conductors' Suite at Tanglewood in honor of Sejii Ozawa's retirement.

THE PAINTINGS IN THIS BOOK

Morgan Bulkeley, Jr.   53
Kingfisher Sketches
Oil on carved maple wood, 12.5 x 10.75 in.
Courtesy of the artist

Emily Buchanan   40
Spring Along the Housatonic (Turnip Island)
Oil on masonite, 12 x 24 in.
Private collection

Thomas Cole (1801–1848)   18
*View of Hoosac Mountain and Pontoosuc Lake
Near Pittsfield, Massachusetts* (c. 1834)
Oil on canvas, 33 x 45 in.
Collection of The Newark Museum
Purchase by exchange, 1988
Gift of Mr. and Mrs. Charles W. Engelhard

Bart Elsbach   51
Housatonic Bend from Kellogg Road
Oil on panel, 10 x 12 in.
Courtesy of the artist

Frank Federico   46
River Bend
Acrylic, 24 x 30 in.
Private collection

Warner Friedman   37
Free Ride to the Housatonic
Acrylic on canvas, 68 x 46 in.
Courtesy of the artist

Edward Gay (1837-1928)   22
Twin Lakes with Cattle (1868)
Oil on canvas, 31 x 54 in.
Courtesy of the Salisbury Association

Ann Getsinger   49
Woman, River, and Bridge
Oil on wood panel, 20 x 24 in.
Courtesy of the artist

Arshile Gorky (1904–1948)   39
Golden Brown (1943-44)
Oil on canvas, 43.8 x 55.6 in.
Courtesy of Washington University Gallery
  of Art, St. Louis
University purchase, Bixby Fund, 1953

Joan Griswold   52
A Lazy River
Oil on canvas, 12 x 16 in.
Courtesy of the artist

Helen Nichols Jacobs   43
Rushing Waters at Bulls Bridge
Oil on canvas, 24 x 30 in.
Courtesy of the artist

Donald Jurney   36
South County Summer (1988)
Oil on panel, 12 x 24 in.
Courtesy of Hoorn–Ashby Gallery, New York

John Manikowski   41
River Pool with Trout
Acrylic on wood, 18 x 24 in.
Courtesy of the artist

David McCandless   47
Housatonic near Glendale
Pastel, 18.5 x 18.5 in.
Courtesy of the artist

George L. K. Morris (1905-1975)   38
Housatonic River
Oil on canvas, 23 x 28 in.
Courtesy Frelinghuysen Morris House and
Studio Collection

Geoffrey Moss   45
Three Beakers
Mixed media on paper, 12 x 12 in.
Courtesy of the artist

Woldemar Neufeld (1909–2002)   50
Housatonic Bridge at Kent (1976)
Watercolor and pen and ink, 14 x 22 in.
Courtesy of the Neufeld Family

Hobart Nichols   24
Housatonic in Winter (1925)
Oil on canvas
Location unknown

June Parker   33
Riverbank
Pastel, 39.5 x 30 in.
Courtesy of the artist

Arthur Parton (1842–1914)   **23**
Scene on the Housatonic River (c.1885)
Oil on canvas, 60 x 42 in.
The Berkshire Museum, Pittsfield

Erica Child Prud'homme   44
Under the Bridge: Spring Melt
Oil on wood panel, 6.75 x 18 in.
Private collection

Jim Schantz   34
September, Housatonic Reflection
Pastel, 48.25 x 48.25 in.
Courtesy of Pucker Gallery, Boston

Gabrielle Senza   42
Il Silenzio di Luce VII
Oil on canvas, 32 x 40 in.
Private collection

Mary Sipp-Green   35
River Lights
Oil on linen, 40 x 52 in.
Courtesy of the artist
Photo: Arthur Evans, Williamstown

Margot Trout   48
Green Bridge
Oil on canvas, 24 x 30 in.
Courtesy of the artist

Anthon Henry Wenzler (d. 1871)   **21**
View of Great Barrington (1849)
Oil on canvas, 45 x 65 in.
The Berkshire Museum, Pittsfield

Most of the etchings in this book are by
J. D. Woodward, from William Cullen Bryant's
"Picturesque America," Volume 2 (1874).
S.V. Hunt's engraving on pages 2 and 3 is
also from that book, after a painting by
A. F. Bellows.

SHEFFIELD ART LEAGUE OF THE BERKSHIRES

Founded in 1974, the Sheffield Art League is a collaborative association of artists and art supporters who promote the creation, appreciation, and support of the fine arts. Members are full- and part-time residents of Berkshire County and nearby New York State and Connecticut. The group welcomes artists from beginners to professional artists, as well as non-artists who appreciate and support art in our world. The Sheffield Art League partners with local historical societies and conservancy associations to co-sponsor events that focus on the art, artists, history, and natural resources of the region. In addition to sponsoring annual juried art shows, the group has an active educational program of art workshops, art demonstrations, lectures, and museum trips, all open to the public, and a scholarship program for high school seniors.

Officers: Nancy Goldberger, President; Bill Connell, Vice President; Hans Heuberger, Treasurer

For more information, see www.SheffieldArtLeague.org

HOUSATONIC RIVER SUMMER 2004

A series of art, river, and cultural events from May to November 2004, Housatonic River Summer aims to raise public awareness of the upper Housatonic River. Under the leadership of the Sheffield Art League more than 30 art, conservancy, cultural, and educational organizations are working together to celebrate the river and the region. Events include juried art, photography, and sculpture shows of work inspired by the Housatonic River, its tributaries, and its flora and fauna; other exhibitions of river artists and river artifacts; workshops on the Housatonic watershed, its ecology and plant life, and its past pollution and cleanup efforts; guided river walks and canoe trips; concerts and lectures on historic contemporary artists and composers inspired by the Housatonic; and river races, flotilla, and festival days. Proceeds raised from Housatonic River Summer events will be used for a river improvement project to increase public access and enjoyment of the river.

Tax-deductible donations may be sent to:
Housatonic River Summer 2004 Fund, Berkshire Taconic Community Foundation, 271 Main Street, Great Barrington, MA 01230

For more information on events and the sponsoring organizations, see www.HousatonicRiverSummer.org